chicken
creative

Chef express

table of contents

Introduction 3

Starters
Chicken and Corn Chowder 6
Chicken and Mango Pasta Salad 10
Chicken Avocado Strudel 14
Chicken Waldorf Loaf 12
Warm Spicy Chicken Green Salad 8

In a Pan
Chicken and Pimento Casserole 26
Chicken Wings Moroccan Style 24
Chicken with Oregano and Lemon 18
Coq au Vin 22
Italian Chicken in a Pan 16
Vineyard Chicken 20

Baked
Chicken and Fresh Herb Terrine 40
Chicken Galantine Slices 38
Chicken with Spinach Filling 32
Crisp Curried Wings 30
Crusty Chicken Goulash 42
Herb Chutney Chicken 34
Rice-filled Chicken 36
Smoked Chicken 28

Fried and Stir-fried
Cajun Chicken Fettuccine 54
Chicken with Garlic and Pepper 44
Chicken with Lime and Coconut 48
Indonesian Chicken 52
Southern-fried Chicken Drumsticks 46
Sweet Chicken Drumsticks with Polenta Crust ... 50

Grilled
Char-grilled Tarragon Chicken 58
Spicy Mango Chicken 60
Thai Lime Spatchcocks 56
Teriyaki Tenderloins 62

introduction

Chicken appeared as an invaluable meal on the tables of ancient Egypt, Greece, Rome and Asia. Today, almost all global cuisines use it one way or another; this is why we have inherited recipes from such diverse origins as Japanese teriyaki, Moroccan wings, or French Coq au Vin, just to name the most popular.

creative chicken
introduction

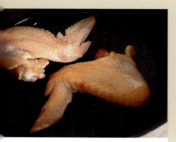

Goes with everything

Far from imposing, its delicate flavor combines well with all side dishes and condiments. Pan-fried with potatoes, in salads with avocado or grilled with lemon, chicken always plays the leading role in meals.

Nutritional values and assets

Rich in protein, essential aminoacids, A and B vitamins, and minerals like iron and zinc, it is easily digested. Range chickens are highly recommended since their meat, superior in flavor and texture, is less fatty, more natural and healthier.

The best choice

The skin of fresh chicken should have an all over yellowish aspect, without bruises, torn parts or excessive moisture. The flesh must be firm, compact and slightly pink colored. When buying frozen chicken make sure the package is intact and no ice has formed, a sign cold storage was interrupted.

How to preserve

Fresh chicken can be stored up to three days in the coolest part of the refrigerator (about 4°C/8°F). When bought frozen, it must be placed immediately in the freezer. It's better to use ground chicken immediately. Once cooked it can be frozen up to six months.

Chicken pieces

- Individual pieces (for stews and casseroles)
- Whole breasts (for barbecues or oven grilled)
- Boneless breasts (for pan-frying)
- Drumsticks (breaded and fried)
- Ground (for hamburgers, terrines or fillings)
- Strips (for oriental stir-fries)
- Wings (for crunchy snacks)
- Boneless thighs (for filling)

With or without skin?

For certain recipes, or when cooking low fat meals, chicken skin must be removed. Leave it on when cooking chicken in salt, spit roaster, or by the typical Argentine country technique consisting in covering chicken with fragrant herbs and wet clay before roasting. For famous French dish poularde demi deuil, with truffle slices stuffed under the skin, or when making slow cooking stews and casseroles, skin must also be left on.

Difficulty scale

■☐☐ I Easy to do

■■☐ I Requires attention

■■■ I Requires experience

6 > CREATIVE CHICKEN

chicken
and corn chowder

■ □ □ | Cooking time: 21 minutes - Preparation time: 25 minutes

ingredients
- 1 tablespoon vegetable oil
- 1 small onion, diced
- 250 g/8 oz boneless chicken breast fillets, shredded
- 3 potatoes, chopped
- 3 1/2 cups/875 ml/1 1/2 pt chicken stock
- 315 g/10 oz canned sweet corn kernels, drained and coarsely chopped
- 1 1/4 cups/315 ml/10 fl oz milk
- 1 bay leaf
- freshly ground black pepper
- 1 tablespoon lemon juice
- 2 tablespoons chopped fresh parsley
- 1 tablespoon snipped fresh chives
- 60 g/2 oz grated Parmesan cheese

method
1. Heat oil in a saucepan over a medium heat, add onion and cook, stirring, for 4-5 minutes or until onion is soft. Add chicken and cook for 2 minutes longer or until chicken just changes color.
2. Add potatoes and stock and bring to the boil. Reduce heat and simmer for 10 minutes or until potatoes are almost cooked. Stir sweet corn, milk, bay leaf and black pepper to taste into stock mixture and bring to the boil. Reduce heat and simmer for 3-4 minutes or until potatoes are cooked. Remove bay leaf. Stir in lemon juice, parsley, chives and black pepper to taste. Just prior to serving, sprinkle with Parmesan cheese.

....
Serves 6

tip from the chef
To chop sweet corn, place in a food processor or blender and process using the pulse button until coarsely chopped. Creamed sweet corn can be used in place of the kernels if you wish. If using creamed sweet corn there is no need to chop it.

starters > 7

starters > 9

warm spicy chicken green salad

Cooking time: 10 minutes - Preparation time: 30 minutes

method

1. Melt butter in a frying pan over a high heat and stir-fry chicken on both sides. Season with salt, pour in balsamic vinegar and cook till reduced. Stand.
2. To make dressing, combine honey with vinegar and salt in a bowl, whisk to combine. Add chives, peach and half of the chilies, add oil beating until smooth.
3. On a serving platter make a bed with rocket, endive and lettuce. Place chicken and snow peas on top. Drizzle with dressing and garnish with remaining chilies.

Serves 4

ingredients

- 60 g/2 oz butter
- 4 boneless chicken breasts fillets, cooked and sliced
- salt
- 1/4 cup balsamic vinegar
- 200 g/7 oz snow peas, cooked
- rocket, curly endives and lettuce leaves, washed and drained

hot dressing

- 1 tablespoon honey
- 1/8 cup balsamic vinegar
- 1 teaspoon salt
- 2 tablespoons snipped chives
- 1 peach, stoned, peeled and finely chopped
- 4 fresh chilies, diagonally sliced
- 1/2 cup olive oil

tip from the chef

This salad can be served in winter as well as summer. Makes for a perfect starter or as a main dish, depending on the occasion.

10 > CREATIVE CHICKEN

chicken
and mango pasta salad

starters > 11

■☐☐ | Cooking time: 8-10 minutes - Preparation time: 10 minutes

method
1. Cook pasta in boiling water in a large saucepan following packet directions. Drain, rinse under cold running water and drain again.
2. Place pasta, chicken, water chestnuts and mangoes in a bowl and toss to combine.
3. To make dressing, place mayonnaise, chutney, spring onions, coriander and black pepper to taste in a bowl and mix to combine. Spoon dressing over salad and toss to combine. Cover and chill until required.

Serves 6

ingredients
- 500 g/1 lb large shell pasta
- 1 cooked chicken, flesh cut into bite-sized pieces
- 220 g/7 oz canned water chestnuts, drained and sliced
- 440 g/14 oz canned mangoes, drained and sliced

mango chutney dressing
- 1 cup/250 g/8 oz low-oil mayonnaise
- 1/2 cup/155 g/5 oz sweet mango chutney
- 2 spring onions, finely chopped
- 2 tablespoons chopped fresh coriander
- freshly ground black pepper

tip from the chef
Chicken salads are a great addition to a buffet or one such as this is a substantial one-dish meal. Leftover cooked turkey is a tasty alternative to chicken and when fresh mangoes are in season use these rather than canned ones.

chicken waldorf loaf

■□□ | Cooking time: 0 minutes - Preparation time: 30 minutes

ingredients
- 1 cottage loaf
- 1 Granny Smith apple, finely chopped
- 60 g/2 oz walnuts, chopped
- 3 spring onions, finely chopped
- 2 tablespoons chopped fresh parsley
- 1/2 cup/125 g/4 oz mayonnaise
- freshly ground black pepper
- 10 spinach leaves, stalks removed
- 3 boneless chicken breast fillets, cooked and sliced
- 4 tomatoes, sliced

method
1. Cut top off the loaf and scoop out middle, so that only the crust remains as a large bread case. Reserve top of loaf. The crumbs from the center will not be used in this recipe, but can be made into bread crumbs.
2. Place apple, walnuts, spring onions, parsley, mayonnaise and black pepper to taste in a bowl and mix to combine. Place a layer of spinach leaves in base of bread case, top with a layer of chicken, a layer of apple mixture and finally a layer of tomato slices. Repeat layers, ending with a layer of spinach, until all ingredients are used and loaf is filled. Replace top and wrap loaf in aluminum foil. Place a board on top of loaf, weight down and refrigerate overnight. Serve cut into wedges.

Serves 8

tip from the chef
This can also be a perfect picnic dish – delicate chicken breasts are combined with Waldorf salad ingredients, placed in a bread case, wrapped in aluminum foil and refrigerated overnight. All you have to do in the morning is pack the picnic basket and you are ready to go.

starters > 13

14 > CREATIVE CHICKEN

chicken
avocado strudel

starters > 15

■ ☐ ☐ | Cooking time: 35 minutes - Preparation time: 25 minutes

method
1. To make filling, heat oil in a frying pan and cook onion and curry powder for 4-5 minutes or until onion is soft. Transfer onion mixture to a bowl, add cream cheese, chicken, red pepper, mushrooms, avocado and black pepper to taste. Mix well to combine.
2. Layer filo pastry sheets on top of each other, brushing between layers with oil. Top pastry with chicken mixture and roll up tightly, tucking ends under. Place on a baking tray, brush with oil, sprinkle with sesame seeds and bake at 180°C/350°F/Gas 4 for 30 minutes or until golden.

Serves 6

ingredients
> 10 sheets filo pastry
> 4 tablespoons vegetable oil
> 2 tablespoons sesame seeds

chicken avocado filling
> 1 tablespoon oil
> 1 small onion, chopped
> 2 teaspoons curry powder
> 200 g/6 1/2 oz cream cheese, softened
> 2 chicken breast fillets, cooked and cut into strips
> 1/2 red pepper, sliced
> 8 button mushrooms, sliced
> 1 avocado, stoned, peeled and sliced
> freshly ground black pepper

tip from the chef
For a lower calorie version, ricotta cheese can be used instead of cream cheese.

italian
chicken in a pan

■□□ | Cooking time: 15 minutes - Preparation time: 15 minutes

ingredients
> 6 boneless chicken breast fillets, skinned
> seasoned flour
> 1 egg, beaten
> dried breadcrumbs
> 1/4 cup/60 ml/2 fl oz vegetable oil
> 500 g/1 lb bottled tomato pasta sauce
> 6 slices prosciutto or ham
> 6 slices mozzarella cheese
> 6 sprigs fresh sage

tip from the chef
In this recipe, fresh sliced tomatoes placed under the mozzarella sheets can be used instead of the bottled tomato sauce.

method
1. Place chicken between sheets of greaseproof paper and pound lightly to flatten. Dust with flour, then dip in egg and finally coat with breadcrumbs (a). Place on a plate lined with plastic food wrap and refrigerate for 15 minutes.
2. Heat oil in a large frying pan over a medium heat, add chicken and cook for 2-3 minutes each side (b) or until golden. Remove from pan and set aside.
3. Add pasta sauce to pan and cook over a medium heat, stirring, for 4-5 minutes or until hot. Place chicken in a single layer on top of sauce, then top each fillet with a slice of prosciutto or ham, a slice of cheese (c) and a sprig of sage. Cover and simmer for 5 minutes or until chicken is cooked through and cheese melts. Serve immediately.

Serves 6

a

b

c

 in a pan > 17

chicken
with oregano and lemon

in a pan

> 19

■☐☐ | Cooking time: 25 minutes - Preparation time: 20 minutes

method
1. Season chicken with dried oregano, pepper and salt.
2. Heat oil in a large fry pan.
3. Add chicken, potatoes and onions, and brown quickly for 2-3 minutes.
4. Pour in stock, cover, and simmer for 10-15 minutes or until chicken is cooked.
5. Add lemon juice and fresh oregano. Season to taste. Cook for 3 minutes longer. Serve immediately.

Serves 4

ingredients
> 4 chicken breasts
> 2 teaspoons dried oregano
> freshly ground pepper and salt
> 2 tablespoons olive oil
> 600 g/20 oz potatoes, sliced to 5 mm/$1/5$ in
> 1 bunch spring onions, trimmed and halved
> 125 ml/4 fl oz chicken stock
> 75 ml/$2^{1/2}$ fl oz lemon juice
> 2 sprigs oregano, chopped

tip from the chef
This recipe is delicious when fresh herbs are used. It's always good to have a plant, even if it is on a window box in the kitchen.

> CREATIVE CHICKEN

vineyard chicken

■■□ | Cooking time: 35 minutes - Preparation time: 30 minutes

ingredients

> 4 boneless chicken breast or thigh fillets
> 2 teaspoons vegetable oil
> 2 onions, sliced
> 2 cloves garlic, crushed
> 440 g/14 oz canned tomatoes, undrained and mashed
> 1 green pepper, chopped
> 1 cup/250 ml/4 fl oz dry white wine

ricotta filling

> 125 g/4 oz ricotta cheese, drained
> 2 tablespoons chopped fresh basil
> freshly ground black pepper

method

1. Make a deep slit in the side of each chicken fillet to form a pocket.
2. To make filling, place ricotta cheese, basil and black pepper to taste in a bowl and mix to combine. Fill pockets with filling (a) and secure with toothpicks.
3. Heat oil in a large frying pan, add onions and garlic and cook, stirring, for 3 minutes or until onions are soft. Add tomatoes (b), green pepper and wine (c) to pan and cook, stirring, for 2 minutes.
4. Add chicken to pan (d), cover and simmer, turning chicken occasionally, for 30 minutes or until chicken is tender.

Serves 4

tip from the chef

This recipe can be completed to the end of step 2 several hours in advance.

a

b

c

in a pan > 21

d

> CREATIVE CHICKEN

coq au vin

in a pan > 23

■■□ | Cooking time: 100 minutes - Preparation time: 10 minutes

method
1. Toss chicken in flour to coat. Shake off excess flour and set aside.
2. Heat oil in a large, nonstick frying pan over a medium heat and cook chicken in batches, turning frequently, for 10 minutes or until brown on all sides. Remove chicken from pan and drain on absorbent kitchen paper.
3. Add garlic, onions or shallots and bacon to pan and cook, stirring, for 5 minutes or until onions are golden. Return chicken to pan, stir in stock and wine and bring to the boil. Reduce heat, cover and simmer, stirring occasionally, for 1¼ hours or until chicken in tender. Add mushrooms and black pepper to taste and cook for 10 minutes longer.

ingredients
> 2 kg/4 lb chicken pieces
> ½ cup/60 g/2 oz seasoned flour
> 2 tablespoons olive oil
> 2 cloves garlic, crushed
> 12 pickling onions or shallots, peeled
> 8 rashers bacon, chopped
> 1 cup/250 ml/8 fl oz chicken stock
> 3 cups/750 ml/1¼ pt red wine
> 250 g/8 oz button mushrooms
> freshly ground black pepper

Serves 6

tip from the chef
Wine is a natural flavor essential for the meat. For that reason, only good quality wines should be used in this and all recipes.

chicken
wings moroccan style

Cooking time: 55 minutes - Preparation time: 15 minutes

ingredients
- 2 tablespoons oil
- 1 kg/2 lb tray chicken wings
- 1 large onion, finely chopped
- 1 clove garlic, crushed
- 1 1/2 teaspoons chopped fresh ginger
- 1/2 teaspoon ground turmeric
- 1/2 teaspoon cumin
- 1/2 cinnamon stick
- 1/4 cup/60 ml/2 fl oz cider vinegar
- 450 g/15 oz canned apricot nectar
- salt, pepper
- 100 g/3 oz dried prunes, pitted
- 100 g/3 oz dried apricots
- 1 tablespoon honey
- 1/4 cup/60 ml/2 fl oz lemon juice
- steamed couscous or rice to serve

method
1. Heat oil in a wide-based saucepan or lidded skillet, add chicken wings a few at a time (a) and brown lightly on both sides. Remove to a plate as they brown.
2. Add onions and fry for 2 minutes (b). Stir in garlic, ginger and spices. Cook while stirring for 1 minute, return chicken to the pan, stir and turn the wings to coat with spices. Add vinegar and apricot nectar (c), season to taste. Cover and simmer for 25 minutes.
3. Add prunes, apricots, honey and lemon juice (d). Cover and simmer 10 minutes and then remove lid and simmer uncovered for 5 minutes. If a thicker sauce is desired, remove wings and fruit to a serving platter, increase heat and boil until sauce reduces and thickens, stirring occasionally. Pour sauce over wings. Serve immediately with steamed couscous or rice.

Serves 3-4

tip from the chef
For a more substantial meal, replace the chicken wings for drumsticks.

a

in a pan > 25

b c d

chicken
and pimento casserole

in a pan > 27

■■□ | Cooking time: 23 minutes - Preparation time: 22 minutes

method
1. Heat oil in a large frying pan and cook chicken, stirring, over a medium heat for 2-3 minutes (a) or until chicken just changes color. Remove chicken from pan and set aside.
2. Add turnip, onions and pimentos to frying pan and cook for 3-4 minutes. Stir in wine (b) and tomatoes and bring to the boil, stirring, over a medium heat, then reduce heat and simmer, uncovered, for 10 minutes or until turnip is tender. Return chicken to pan and cook for 3-4 minutes longer (c) or until chicken is cooked. Stir in basil and serve immediately.

ingredients
> 2 tablespoons vegetable oil
> 4 boneless chicken breast fillets, cut into strips
> 1 turnip, cut into strips
> 2 onions, chopped
> 440 g/14 oz canned pimentos, drained and cut into strips
> 1 cup/250 ml/8 fl oz dry white wine
> 440 g/14 oz canned tomatoes, undrained and mashed
> 3 tablespoons chopped fresh basil

Serves 4

tip from the chef
All this easy chicken dish needs to make a complete meal is hot garlic bread or crusty bread rolls and a salad of mixed lettuce and herbs.

a

b

c

smoked chicken

■☐☐ | Cooking time: 80 minutes - Preparation time: 5 minutes

ingredients
- 1/2 cup/125 g/4 oz sugar
- 3 tablespoons tea leaves
- 2 tablespoons salt
- 1 x 1.5 kg/3 lb chicken
- freshly ground black pepper
- 1 tablespoon soy sauce
- 2 teaspoons sesame oil

method
1. Line a baking dish with sheets of aluminum foil large enough to completely enclose the chicken. Combine sugar, tea leaves and salt and spread out over foil. Place a roasting rack in the baking dish and place chicken on rack. Sprinkle chicken liberally with black pepper, bring foil up around chicken to completely enclose and bake at 190°C/375°F/Gas 5 for 1 hour.
2. Combine soy sauce and sesame oil. Open foil parcel, brush chicken with soy sauce mixture and bake, uncovered, for 20 minutes longer or until chicken is cooked through. To serve, cut into pieces and serve immediately.

Serves 6

tip from the chef
Chicken cooked in this way is moist with a crisp skin and distinctive flavor.

baked > 29

baked > 31

crisp curried wings

■■□ | Cooking time: 70 minutes - Preparation time: 30 minutes

method

1. Rinse the chicken wings and pat dry with kitchen paper. Rub the curry paste well onto the chicken wings with your fingers, covering all surfaces. Pin back the wing tip to form a triangle. Place in single layer on a tray; stand for 30 minutes in refrigerator, uncovered.
2. Meanwhile place the rice in a 8 cup/2 lt/ 70 fl oz casserole dish; add salt and boiling water. Cover with lid or foil and place on lower shelf oven, preheated at 180°C/350°F/Gas 4. Cook for 40 minutes. Remove from oven and stand, covered, 5 minutes.
3. Transfer chicken wings to a wire rack placed over a baking tray. Place on top shelf of oven above the rice. Cook for 20 minutes, turning once. When rice has been removed, increase oven temperature to 200°C/400°F/Gas 6 for 5 minutes to crisp the wings.
4. Halve the tomatoes and remove the seeds then cut into small dice. Peel cucumber; slice in half lengthwise, remove the seeds with a teaspoon. Dice the cucumber and mix with the diced tomato. Place in a suitable dish, place chutney in a similar dish. Serve the crisp curried wings with the rice and accompanying sambals.

Serves 4-6

ingredients

> 1 kg/2 lb chicken wings
> 2 tablespoons mild curry paste
> 1 1/2 cups/330 g/11 oz basmati rice, rinsed
> 1/2 teaspoon salt
> 3 cups/750 ml/1 1/4 pt boiling water
> 2 tomatoes, blanched and skinned
> 1 small cucumber
> 1 cup/240 g/8 oz fruit chutney

tip from the chef

Co-ordinate the cooking so that rice and chicken utilize the same oven.

32 > CREATIVE CHICKEN

chicken
with spinach filling

a b c

baked > 33

■■□ | Cooking time: 44 minutes - Preparation time: 15 minutes

method

1. To make filling, squeeze spinach (a) to remove excess liquid. Place spinach, garlic, ricotta or cottage cheese, Parmesan cheese, lemon rind and nutmeg in a bowl and mix to combine.
2. Using your fingers, loosen skin on chicken (b), starting at thigh end.
3. Push filling gently under skin down into the drumstick (c). Arrange chicken pieces in an ovenproof dish, brush with melted butter and bake at 180°C/350°F/Gas 4 for 35-40 minutes.
4. To make sauce, place tomato purée and Worcestershire sauce in a saucepan, bring to simmering and simmer for 3-4 minutes. Serve sauce with chicken.

Serves 4

ingredients

> **4 chicken marylands (uncut leg and thigh joints)**
> **30 g/1 oz butter, melted**

spinach filling
> **125 g/4 oz frozen spinach, thawed**
> **1 clove garlic, crushed**
> **125 g/4 oz ricotta or cottage cheese, drained**
> **2 teaspoons grated Parmesan cheese**
> **1 teaspoon finely grated lemon rind**
> **pinch ground nutmeg**

tomato sauce
> **310 g/10 oz canned tomato purée**
> **2 teaspoons Worcestershire sauce**

tip from the chef

Drumsticks can be used in place of the chicken marylands. Frozen chicken should be completely thawed before cooking. Thaw birds in refrigerator for 24-36 hours or in microwave on Defrost (30%) for 10-15 minutes per 500 g/1 lb of chicken. Rinse cavity of chicken under cold running water to ensure that there are no remaining ice crystals.

herb
chutney chicken

■ ☐ ☐ | Cooking time: 90 minutes - Preparation time: 15 minutes

ingredients
> 1 x 1.5 kg/3 lb chicken
> 60 g/2 oz butter, melted
> 2 cloves garlic, crushed

chutney stuffing
> 2 tablespoons chopped fresh mixed herbs such as parsley, chives, rosemary, thyme and oregano
> 125 g/4 oz grated fresh Parmesan cheese
> 2 tablespoons fruit chutney
> 1 egg, lightly beaten
> 1 cup/60 g/2 oz dried bread crumbs
> 90 g/3 oz butter, melted

method
1. To make stuffing, place herbs, Parmesan cheese, chutney, egg, bread crumbs and butter in a bowl and mix to combine. Fill cavity of chicken with stuffing and secure opening with metal or bamboo skewers.
2. Tuck wings under body of chicken and tie legs together. Place bird breast side up in a baking dish. Combine butter and garlic, brush over chicken and bake at 180°C/350°F/Gas 4, turning several times, for 1-1½ hours or until bird is cooked.

Serves 4

tip from the chef
When making stuffing, try doubling the quantity and cooking the remainder in a dish to serve as extra stuffing with the bird. Or use to fill vegetables such as tomatoes and red and green peppers. These vegetables will take 20-30 minutes to cook and can be baked with the chicken.

baked > 35

36 > CREATIVE CHICKEN

baked

rice-filled
chicken

■■■ | Cooking time: 110 minutes - Preparation time: 40 minutes

method

1. Using absorbent kitchen paper, pat chicken dry inside and out. Cook bacon, spring onions and curry powder in a frying pan over a medium heat for 4-5 minutes or until bacon is crisp. Remove pan from heat and stir in rice and bread crumbs.
2. Fill cavity of chicken with rice mixture and secure opening with metal or bamboo skewers. Tuck wings under body of chicken and tie legs together. Place bird breast side up in a baking dish. Brush with oil and bake at 180°C/350°F/Gas 4, basting frequently with pan juices, for 1½ hours or until bird is cooked.
3. To make sauce, melt butter in a saucepan and cook onion, green pepper and mushrooms for 2-3 minutes. Stir in tomatoes, tomato paste (purée), wine, sugar, water and black pepper to taste. Cook, stirring constantly, over a medium heat for 10-15 minutes or until sauce is reduced by a quarter. Serve sauce with chicken.

Serves 4

ingredients

> 1 x 1.5 kg/3 lb chicken, cleaned
> 4 rashers bacon, chopped
> 4 spring onions, chopped
> 2 teaspoons curry powder
> ¾ cup/170 g/5½ oz long-grain rice, cooked
> 1 cup/60 g/2 oz bread crumbs, made from stale bread
> 1 tablespoon olive oil

mushroom sauce

> 30 g/1 oz butter
> 1 onion, chopped
> 1 green pepper, chopped
> 125 g/4 oz mushrooms, sliced
> 440 g/14 oz canned tomatoes, undrained and mashed
> 2 tablespoons tomato paste (purée)
> 3 tablespoons red wine
> 1 tablespoon sugar
> ½ cup/125 ml/4 fl oz water
> freshly ground black pepper

tip from the chef

To test when a bird is cooked, place a skewer into the thickest part of the thigh. If juices run clear, bird is ready. If they are tinged pink, cook for 15 minutes longer, then test again. On completion of cooking, allow whole birds to stand in a warm place for 10-20 minutes before carving. This tenderizes the meat by allowing the juices to settle into the flesh.

chicken
galantine slices

baked

■■□ | Cooking time: 45 minutes - Preparation time: 35 minutes

method

1. To make filling, place chicken and sausage minces, onion, parsley, garlic, egg and black pepper to taste in a bowl and mix to combine.
2. Place each chicken breast fillet, cut side up, on a flat surface between sheets of plastic food wrap and pound lightly to make a flattened rectangle. Lay 3 slices prosciutto or ham over each rectangle. Place one-sixth of the filling lengthwise down the center, top with a row of 5 prunes and cover with another one-sixth of the filling.
3. Wrap fillets around filling to enclose and tie at 2 cm/³⁄₄ in intervals with kitchen string. Wrap rolls in light buttered aluminum foil and place in a baking dish.
4. Bake at 180°C/350°F/Gas 4 for 30 minutes, remove rolls from foil and bake for 15 minutes or until chicken is cooked. Wrap rolls in clean aluminum foil and refrigerate for several hours or until cold. To serve, remove string and cut into 1 cm/½ in thick slices.

ingredients

- 3 double boneless chicken breast fillets
- 9 slices prosciutto or lean ham
- 15 pitted dessert prunes

savory filling

- 375 g/12 oz chicken mince
- 200 g/6½ oz sausage mince
- 1 onion, finely chopped
- 3-4 tablespoons chopped fresh parsley
- 2 cloves garlic, crushed
- 1 egg, lightly beaten
- freshly ground black pepper

Makes about 45

tip from the chef

This dish can make for a magnificent starter or for a complete summertime meal, next to a salad.

chicken
and fresh herb terrine

■ ■ □ | Cooking time: 125 minutes - Preparation time: 40 minutes

ingredients
- 1 bunch/500 g/1 lb spinach or silverbeet
- 250 g/8 oz chicken livers, cleaned
- 1 tablespoon seasoned flour
- 15 g/1 oz butter
- 1 teaspoon olive oil
- 375 g/12 oz chicken meat, a mixture of white and dark meat, ground
- 375 g/12 oz lean pork, ground
- 2 teaspoons finely chopped fresh thyme or 1 teaspoon dried thyme
- 3 cloves garlic, crushed
- 2 onions, diced
- 1 tablespoon green peppercorns in brine, drained
- 3 eggs
- 1/2 cup/125 ml/4 fl oz dry white wine
- 2 tablespoons port or sherry
- 3 tablespoons chopped fresh parsley
- freshly ground black pepper

method
1. Preheat oven. Boil, steam or microwave spinach or silverbeet leaves to soften. Drain; refresh under cold running water and drain again. Line a lightly greased terrine dish or an 11 x 21 cm/4$^{1/2}$ x 8$^{1/2}$ in loaf tin with overlapping spinach leaves. Allow leaves to overhang the sides.
2. Toss chicken livers in seasoned flour to coat. Heat butter and oil in a frying pan over a medium heat until foaming. Add chicken livers and cook, stirring, for 3-5 minutes or until they just change color. Remove livers from pan and set aside to cool.
3. Chop chicken livers. Place chicken livers, chicken, pork, thyme, garlic, onions, green peppercorns, eggs, wine, port or sherry, parsley and black pepper to taste in a bowl and mix to combine.
4. Pack meat mixture into prepared terrine dish or loaf tin, fold overhanging spinach leaves over filling and cover with aluminum foil. Place terrine dish of loaf in a baking dish with enough boiling water to come halfway up the sides of the dish and bake at 180°C/350°F/Gas 4 for 2 hours. Drain off juices, cover top of terrine with foil, then weight and set aside to cool. When cold, refrigerate overnight. To serve, unmold and cut into slices.

Serves 10

baked > 41

42 > CREATIVE CHICKEN

crusty
chicken goulash

a   b   c

baked > 43

■□□ | Cooking time: 60 minutes - Preparation time: 10 minutes

method

1. Heat 1 tablespoon oil in a large frying pan and cook onions, stirring, over a medium heat for 5-6 minutes or until golden. Remove onions from pan and set aside. Combine paprika and flour in a plastic food bag, add chicken, shake to coat with flour mixture, then shake off excess flour mixture.

2. Heat remaining oil in frying pan and cook chicken, stirring, over a medium heat for 2-3 minutes. Return onions to pan, stir in tomato paste (purée), wine and stock. Bring to the boil, stirring constantly, then reduce heat, cover and simmer for 6-7 minutes. Remove from heat, stir in yogurt and cool.

3. To make crust, place butter, sour cream and egg in a bowl. Stir in flour and parsley and mix well to combine (a).

4. To assemble, place crust mixture in an 8 cup/2 liter/3¹/2 pt lightly greased casserole dish and work mixture to cover sides and base of dish (b).

5. Spoon filling into crust (c), cover with lid of dish and bake at 180°C/350°F/Gas 4 for 35 minutes. Remove lid and bake for 10 minutes longer.

ingredients

> **2 tablespoons vegetable oil**
> **2 large onions, chopped**
> **1¹/2 tablespoons paprika**
> **2 tablespoons seasoned flour**
> **500 g/1 lb boneless chicken breast fillets, cut into strips**
> **1 tablespoon tomato paste (purée)**
> **¹/2 cup/125 ml/4 fl oz red wine**
> **¹/2 cup/125 ml/4 fl oz chicken stock**
> **3 tablespoons natural yogurt**

sour cream crust

> **125 g/4 oz butter, softened**
> **300 g/9¹/2 oz sour cream**
> **1 egg**
> **1 cup/125 g/4 oz self-raising flour, sifted**
> **1 tablespoon chopped fresh parsley**

Serves 4

tip from the chef

A chicken goulash surrounded by a rich sour cream crust is just the thing for that special occasion. Serve this delicious chicken with a tossed green salad or boiled, steamed or microwaved green vegetables such as green beans, zucchini, snow peas or asparagus.

chicken
with garlic and pepper

■□□ | Cooking time: 5 minutes - Preparation time: 10 minutes

ingredients
- 4 cloves garlic
- 3 fresh coriander roots
- 1 teaspoon crushed black peppercorns
- 500 g/1 lb chicken breast fillets, chopped into 3 cm/1 1/4 in cubes
- vegetable oil for deep-frying
- 30 g/1 oz fresh basil leaves
- 30 g/1 oz fresh mint leaves
- sweet chili sauce

method
1. Place garlic, coriander roots and black peppercorns in a food processor and process to make a paste. Coat chicken with garlic paste and marinate for 1 hour.
2. Heat oil in a wok or frying pan over a high heat until a cube of bread dropped in browns in 50 seconds, then deep-fry chicken, a few pieces at a time, for 2 minutes or until golden and tender. Drain on absorbent kitchen paper.
3. Deep-fry basil and mint until crisp, then drain and place on a serving plate. Top with chicken and serve with chili sauce.

Serves 4

tip from the chef
Thai cooks use three types of basil in cooking —Asian sweet, holy and lemon – each has a distinctive flavor and is used for specific types of dishes. For this dish, Asian sweet basil, known in Thailand as horapa, would be used.

fried and stir-fried > 45

46 > CREATIVE CHICKEN

southern-fried
chicken drumsticks

a

b

fried and stir-fried > 47

■ ☐ ☐ | Cooking time: 35 minutes - Preparation time: 10 minutes

method
1. Rinse drumsticks and pat dry with paper towel. Smooth skin over the drumsticks.
2. Mix flour, salt and pepper (a), place on paper-lined, flat plate. Beat eggs and milk well together in a deep plate.
3. Dip the drumsticks in the flour (b) then into the egg, turning to coat both sides. Place again in the flour, lift end of paper to toss flour over drumstick and roll in flour until well covered. Place in single layer on a clean, flat tray.
4. Heat oil in a large frying pan. Add drumsticks and fry a few minutes on each side (c) until just beginning to color. Reduce heat, place a lid on the pan and cook slowly for 20 minutes, turning chicken after 10 minutes (d).
5. Remove lid and increase heat, continue cooking until golden brown and crisp, turning frequently. Remove from pan, drain on paper towels (e). Serve hot with vegetable accompaniments.

ingredients
> 1 kg/2 lb chicken drumsticks
> 1 1/2 cups/180 g/6 fl oz flour
> 1 teaspoon salt and pepper
> 2 eggs
> 1/3 cup/80 ml/3 fl oz milk
> 1/2 cup/120 ml/4 fl oz canola oil

tip from the chef
Pan-fried chicken is a temptation for grown-ups and children alike. It goes fantastic with a three color mash (potato, pumpkin and spinach).

Serves 4

c

d

e

chicken
with lime and coconut

■ ☐ ☐ | Cooking time: 20 minutes - Preparation time: 10 minutes

ingredients
- 1 kg/2 lb chicken thigh or breast fillets, cut into thick strips
- 1 tablespoon Thai red curry paste
- 1 tablespoon vegetable oil
- 3 tablespoons palm or brown sugar
- 4 kaffir lime leaves
- 2 teaspoons finely grated lime rind
- 1 cup/250 ml/8 fl oz coconut cream
- 1 tablespoon Thai fish sauce (nam pla)
- 2 tablespoons coconut vinegar
- 3 tablespoons shredded coconut
- 4 fresh red chilies, sliced

method
1. Place chicken and curry paste in a bowl and toss to coat. Heat oil in a wok or large saucepan over a high heat, add chicken and stir-fry for 4-5 minutes or until lightly browned and fragrant.
2. Add sugar, lime leaves, lime rind, coconut cream and fish sauce and cook, stirring, over a medium heat for 3-4 minutes or until the sugar dissolves and caramelizes.
3. Stir in vinegar and coconut and simmer until chicken is tender. Serve with chilies in a dish on the side.

Serves 4

tip from the chef
For something a little different, serve this dish with egg noodles.

fried and stir-fried > 49

50 > CREATIVE CHICKEN

sweet chicken
drumsticks with

fried and stir-fried > 51

polenta crust

■ ☐ ☐ | Cooking time: 20 minutes - Preparation time: 10 minutes

method
1. Brush each drumstick with the jam, then roll in the flour. Coat with the beaten eggs, then roll in the combined extra flour, salt and polenta, and coat well.
2. Deep-fry drumsticks until golden and cooked through (about 20 minutes).

Serves 4

ingredients
> 8 chicken drumsticks
> 1/4 cup/60 g/2 oz apricot jam (jelly)
> 1 cup/120 g/4 oz plain flour
> 2 eggs, beaten
> 1/2 cup/60 g/2 oz flour, extra
> 1 tablespoon salt
> 3/4 cup/90 g/3 oz polenta
> oil for deep-frying

tip from the chef
Polenta is used more and more in Latin fusion dishes. In this case, it's the perfect coating for this sweet chicken.

indonesian chicken

Cooking time: 15 minutes - **Preparation time:** 15 minutes

ingredients
- 3 tablespoons vegetable oil
- 4 boneless chicken breast fillets, cut into 2 cm/ 3/4 in cubes
- 250 g/8 oz green beans, cut into 2.5 cm/1 in pieces
- 1/4 cup/60 ml/2 fl oz lemon juice
- 2 tablespoons soy sauce
- 1 tablespoon brown sugar
- 2 teaspoons ground turmeric
- 1/2 cup/125 ml/4 fl oz water

method
1. Heat oil in a wok or frying pan, add chicken (a) and stir-fry for 3-4 minutes or until chicken browns. Remove chicken from pan and set aside.
2. Add beans to pan and stir-fry for 2 minutes. Stir in lemon juice, soy sauce (b), sugar, turmeric and water, bring to the boil and simmer for 3-5 minutes or until sauce reduces and thickens slightly. Return chicken to pan and cook for 2-3 minutes longer (c) or until chicken is cooked through.

Serves 4

tip from the chef
For successful stir-frying, heat your wok until very hot, then add the oil. Swirl the wok to coat the surface and continue to heat until the oil is almost smoking before adding the food. This will ensure that the food does not stick to the wok. An exception to this is when the first ingredients to be stir-fried are garlic, spring onions, ginger or chilies. Add these ingredients immediately after the oil or they will burn.

a

b

c

fried and stir-fried > 53

54 > CREATIVE CHICKEN

fried and stir-fried > 55

cajun chicken fettuccine

■■■□ | Cooking time: 20 minutes - Preparation time: 20 minutes

method

1. To make salsa, place tomatoes, chilies, green pepper, sugar and vinegar in a bowl and toss to combine. Set aside.
2. Place paprika, garlic, black peppercorns, cumin, coriander and chili powder in a bowl and mix to combine. Add chicken and toss to coat with spice mixture. Heat oil in a frying pan over a medium heat, add chicken and cook, stirring, for 5 minutes or until chicken is tender. Remove chicken from pan, set aside and keep warm.
3. Cook pasta in boiling water in a large saucepan following packet directions. Drain well and place in a serving dish. Add chicken, toss to combine and serve with salsa.

Serves 8

ingredients

> 2 tablespoons sweet paprika
> 2 cloves garlic, crushed
> 2 teaspoons crushed black peppercorns
> 1 tablespoon ground cumin
> 1 tablespoon ground coriander
> 1/2 teaspoon chili powder
> 6 boneless chicken breast fillets, sliced
> 2 teaspoons vegetable oil
> 750 g/1 1/2 lb fettuccine

tomato salsa

> 6 ripe tomatoes, chopped
> 2 fresh red chilies, seeded and finely chopped
> 1 green pepper, chopped
> 1 tablespoon brown sugar
> 3 tablespoons balsamic or red wine vinegar

tip from the chef

If planning ahead, the salsa can be prepared up to a day in advance. The chicken can be prepared and tossed in the spice mixture several hours in advance, leaving only the cooking of the chicken and pasta to do at the last minute.

> CREATIVE CHICKEN

thai lime
spatchcocks

■□□ | Cooking time: 30 minutes - Preparation time: 10 minutes

ingredients
> 4 small spatchcocks (poussins)

marinade
> 3 tablespoons lime juice
> 2 tablespoons chopped fresh coriander
> 1 cup/250 ml/8 fl oz coconut milk
> 1 red chili, chopped
> 2 tablespoons honey
> freshly ground black pepper

method
1. Cut spatchcocks (poussins) down middle of backs and flatten. Thread a skewer through wings and a skewer through legs of each spatchcock.
2. To make marinade, place lime juice, coriander, coconut milk, chili, honey, and black pepper to taste in a large baking dish. Mix to combine. Place spatchcocks flesh side down in marinade. Cover and refrigerate for 4 hours or overnight.
3. Cook on a hot barbecue or under a hot grill, basting frequently with marinade. Cook 15 minutes each side, or until tender and cooked through.

Serves 4

tip from the chef
As a side dish serve boiled whole wheat, enriched with chives, green peppers and tomato cubes, all seasoned with olive oil, salt and pepper.

grilled > 57

CREATIVE CHICKEN

char-grilled
tarragon chicken

grilled > 59

■ □ □ | Cooking time: 5 minutes - Preparation time: 15 minutes

method

1. Place chicken in a single layer in a shallow glass or ceramic dish. Combine tarragon, wine, lemon rind and green peppercorns. Pour marinade over chicken. Turn to coat chicken with marinade and marinate at room temperature, turning once, for 20 minutes.
2. Remove chicken from marinade and cook on a preheated hot char grill or in a preheated grill pan for 5 minutes or until tender.

ingredients

> 6 boneless chicken breast fillets, skin removed
> 3 tablespoons chopped fresh tarragon or 2 teaspoons dried tarragon
> 1 cup/250 ml/8 fl oz dry white wine
> 2 tablespoons lemon rind strips
> 1 tablespoon green peppercorns in brine, drained and crushed

Serves 6

tip from the chef

Do not marinate chicken any longer than 20 minutes as the marinade will cause the chicken to break down.

60 > CREATIVE CHICKEN

spicy mango chicken

grilled > 61

■■□ | Cooking time: 10 minutes - Preparation time: 40 minutes

method
1. Preheat barbecue to a high heat. Place chicken between sheets of greaseproof paper and pound lightly with a meat mallet to flatten to 1 cm/$^1/_2$ in thick.
2. Combine black pepper, cumin and paprika and sprinkle over chicken. Layer prosciutto or ham and mango slices on chicken, roll up and secure with wooden toothpicks or cocktail sticks. Place chicken on lightly oiled barbecue and cook for 3-5 minutes each side or until chicken is tender and cooked.
3. To make sauce, place mango, garlic, golden syrup and chili sauce in a small saucepan and cook, stirring, over a low heat for 4-5 minutes or until sauce thickens slightly. Serve with chicken.

ingredients
> 4 boneless chicken breast fillets
> 1 teaspoon freshly ground black pepper
> 1 teaspoon ground cumin
> 1 teaspoon paprika
> 4 slices prosciutto or ham, halved
> 2 mangoes, peeled and cut into 2 cm/$^3/_4$ in thick slices

mango sauce
> 1 mango, peeled and chopped
> 1 clove garlic, crushed
> 2 tablespoons golden syrup
> 1 tablespoon sweet chili sauce

Serves 4

tip from the chef
Drained, canned mangoes can be used in place of fresh. You will need two 440 g/14 oz cans of mangoes. Use three-quarters of one can for the sauce and the remainder for the filling in the chicken.

62 > CREATIVE CHICKEN

teriyaki tenderloins

grilled > 63

■ ☐ ☐ | Cooking time: 5 minutes - Preparation time: 5 minutes

method
1. Place tenderloins in a non-metal container and stir in about ¾ cup Teriyaki marinade. Cover and marinate for 30 minutes at room temperature or several hours or overnight in the refrigerator.
2. Heat the barbecue until hot. Place a sheet of baking paper over the grill bars and make a few slits between the bars for ventilation, or place baking paper on the hot plate. Place the tenderloins on grill and cook for 2 minutes on each side until cooked through and golden. Brush with marinade as they cook. Serve immediately with extra Teriyaki marinade as a dipping sauce.

ingredients
> **500 g/1 lb chicken tenderloins**
> **375 g/12½ oz bottle Teriyaki marinade**

Serves 4

tip from the chef
Serving suggestions
- *Serve with steamed rice and vegetables.*
- *Toss into salad greens to make a hot salad. Dress salad with 1 tablespoon Teriyaki marinade, 1 tablespoon vinegar and 3 tablespoons salad oil.*
- *Stuff into heated pocket breads along with shredded lettuce, cucumber and onion rings and drizzle with an extra spoonful of Teriyaki marinade.*

notes

Chef express

family meals

table of contents

Introduction 3

Soups, Pasta and Rice
Bows with Rich Tomato Basil Sauce 14
Cheesy Noodles 16
Minestrone... 10
Spaghetti Basil Soup 6
Spicy Rice Tomato and Vegetables 18
Three Quick Pasta Sauces 12
Vegetable Bean Soup 8

Vegetables
Cauliflower au Gratin 24
Potato Gratin 20
Spinach Roulade 22

Fish
Fish with Italian Sauce 32
Grilled Cod and Potatoes 26
Salmon Cutlets with Pineapple Salsa 28
Snapper Fillets with Lemon and Coriander .. 30

Poultry
Barbecued Chicken and Mushroom Patties.... 40
Chicken Pot Pie 34
Roast Turkey 38
Thigh Steak in Fruity Mint Salsa 36

Meat
Apple Pork Casserole 52
Family Roast 44
Italian Sausage and Pork Roll 46
Lamb and Vegetable Pot 42
Pork and Apple Cabbage Rolls 50
Scotch Meatballs 48

Sweet End
Easy Chocolate Cake 60
Featherlight Scones 58
French Bread Pudding 56
French Vanilla Ice Milk Base 54
Original Choc-chip Cookies 62

introduction

Meal time, especially in the evening, is one of those rare moments of the day in which the family has a chance to get together. That's why this daily little feast deserves our best efforts put to work, to endow it with pleasant moments. A delicious meal, tempting and consistent at the same time, is the one to present to our loved ones.

family meals
introduction

From ancient times, the precedence order at the table has reflected the internal order of the family. Traditions that today are long lost would indicate who was to be served first, who second, as a way of establishing priorities by age and importance.
We could say that the family is formally constituted around the table. What is more, the sense of word home, which designates the house, which connotes family, is not complete without the domestic fire where the food was cooked.

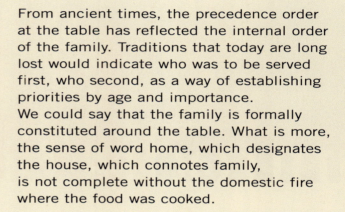

- It is essential that everyday cooking meals be simple, nutritious, easy to make, tempting and suitable for all ages.
- Breads and cereals should not be missing from the daily diet, as they are the basis of the food chain.

- Pasta dishes are perfect when there are teenage members in the house, especially if they practice sports, as they provide carbohydrates, that are assimilated slowly and easily digestible at the same time.
- In the case of a large family, it's better to prepare very abundant dishes, storing individual portions in sealed packages. In time everyone can serve themselves to their liking. This is especially useful when there are children of various ages with diverse schedules and obligations. In this case a microwave oven is of great help, since it enables reheating food easily in a few minutes.
- A generous main dish, fruit or dessert are enough to compose a good homemade meal.
- Stews, soups and oven-cooked dishes are the most convenient, since they are easy to prepare and abundant, usually leaving every one satisfied.

Difficulty scale

■□□ I Easy to do

■■□ I Requires attention

■■■ I Requires experience

spaghetti basil soup

■ □ □ | Cooking time: 27 minutes - Preparation time: 15 minutes

ingredients
- 155 g/5 oz spaghetti, broken into pieces
- 2 tablespoons vegetable oil
- 1 onion, chopped
- 2 cloves garlic, crushed
- 60 g/2 oz slivered almonds
- 4 cups/1 liter/1 3/4 pt chicken stock
- 30 g/1 oz fresh basil leaves, shredded
- freshly ground black pepper

method
1. Cook spaghetti in boiling water in a large saucepan following packet directions. Drain and set aside.
2. Heat oil in a large saucepan and cook onion, garlic and almonds, stirring over a medium heat for 6-7 minutes or until onions are transparent.
3. Add stock and basil to pan and bring to the boil, reduce heat, cover and simmer for 10 minutes. Stir in spaghetti and season to taste with black pepper. Spoon soup into bowls and serve immediately.

Serves 4

tip from the chef
This soup can be frozen because it does not contain eggs or cream. Basil should not be added before freezing the soup, but only on reheating, so that it maintains its properties.

soups, pasta and rice

8 > FAMILY MEALS

vegetable
bean soup

soups, pasta and rice > 9

■☐☐ | Cooking time: 45 minutes - Preparation time: 20 minutes

method
1. Heat oil in a large saucepan over a medium heat, add onions and cook, stirring, for 5 minutes or until onions are lightly browned.
2. Add carrots, potatoes and stock and bring to the boil. Reduce heat, cover and simmer for 30 minutes or until vegetables are tender.
3. Stir in beans, milk, dill, parsley and black pepper to taste and cook, stirring frequently, for 3-4 minutes or until heated through.

Serves 4

ingredients
> 2 tablespoons vegetable oil
> 3 onions, diced
> 3 carrots, diced
> 3 potatoes, diced
> 3 cups/750 ml/1 1/4 pt vegetable stock
> 315 g/10 oz canned cannellini beans, drained and rinsed
> 1/2 cup/125 ml/4 fl oz milk
> 2 tablespoons chopped fresh dill
> 1 tablespoon chopped fresh parsley
> freshly ground black pepper

tip from the chef
It can be served with croûtons (bread cubes, toasted or fried in oil or butter).

10 > FAMILY MEALS

minestrone

■■■ | Cooking time: 95 minutes - Preparation time: 55 minutes

ingredients

> **2 tablespoons/60 g/2 oz butter**
> **2 cloves garlic, crushed**
> **2 small onions, finely chopped**
> **4 rashers bacon, chopped**
> **250 g/8 oz bacon bones**
> **150 g/4^1/2 oz red kidney beans**
> **100 g/3^1/2 oz haricot beans, soaked overnight**
> **^{1}/2 small cabbage, roughly chopped**
> **100 g/3^1/2 oz spinach, washed and chopped**
> **3 medium-sized potatoes, peeled and chopped**
> **2 medium-sized carrots, peeled and diced**
> **150 g/4^1/2 oz fresh (or frozen) peas, shelled**
> **1 stalk celery, chopped**
> **2 tablespoons parsley, finely chopped**
> **2 liters/3^1/2 pt chicken stock**
> **salt to taste**
> **100 g/3^1/2 oz tomato and cheese tortellini**
> **50 g/2 oz pasta of your choice**
> **fresh Parmesan cheese**

method

1. Heat butter and add garlic, onion, bacon and bones. Sauté 4-5 minutes.
2. Add all other ingredients except pasta and bring to the boil. Allow to simmer, covered, for approximately 90 minutes.
3. Remove and discard bacon bones.
4. Stir in both pastas and cook until al dente.

Serves 4

tip from the chef

To serve, sprinkle with a generous helping of Parmesan and a good crusty loaf of your favorite bread.

soups, pasta and rice > 11

12 > FAMILY MEALS

three quick
pasta sauces

soups, pasta and rice

> 13

■□□ | Cooking time: 10 minutes - Preparation time: 10 minutes

method

1. To make tuna sauce, melt butter in a saucepan, add flour and cook for 1 minute. Blend stock and tuna liquid, stirring over medium heat until sauce boils and thickens. Reduce heat and add olives and lemon juice. Season to taste and stir well to combine. Break up tuna into smaller chunks and fold through sauce. Cook for 2-3 minutes. Spoon over hot pasta and serve.

2. To make seafood sauce, heat oil in a saucepan and cook onions for 1 minute. Stir in seafood and cook for 2 minutes longer. Combine tomatoes and wine and pour into pan. Bring to the boil, then reduce heat and simmer, uncovered, for 10 minutes. Add basil and spoon over hot pasta.

3. To make mushroom sauce, heat oil in a frying pan and cook bacon for 3-4 minutes or until crisp. Stir in mushrooms and cook for 2-3 minutes. Pour in cream, bring to the boil, stirring frequently, and simmer for 5 minutes or until sauce thickens. Season to taste, spoon over hot pasta, sprinkle with parsley and serve.

Serves 4

ingredients

tuna and olive sauce
> 30 g/2 oz butter
> 2 tablespoons flour
> 150 ml/5 fl oz chicken stock
> 440 g/14 oz tuna in brine, drained and liquid reserved
> 12 black olives, pitted and sliced
> 2 tablespoons lemon juice

seafood and tomato sauce
> 1 tablespoon olive oil
> 4 spring onions, finely chopped
> 500 g/1 lb assorted seafood, cooked and chopped
> 440 g/14 oz canned tomatoes, undrained and mashed
> 1/2 cup dry white wine
> 1 tablespoon chopped fresh basil

mushroom and bacon sauce
> 2 teaspoons olive oil
> 4 rashers bacon, chopped
> 125 g/4 oz button mushrooms, sliced
> 300 ml/9 fl oz cream (double)
> 1 tablespoon chopped fresh parsley

tip from the chef

For another super quick sauce, heat olive oil with aromatic herbs and condiments: basil, thyme, tarragon, coriander, garlic.

bows with rich tomato basil sauce

■□□ | Cooking time: 30 minutes - Preparation time: 15 minutes

ingredients
> 185 g/6 oz bow pasta

tomato basil sauce
> 2 teaspoons olive oil
> 1 onion, sliced
> 1 clove garlic, crushed
> 3 tomatoes, peeled, seeded and chopped
> 125 ml/4 fl oz chicken stock
> 1 tablespoon tomato purée
> 1 tablespoon chopped fresh basil
> 2 teaspoons chopped fresh parsley
> 1/2 teaspoon sugar
> freshly ground black pepper
> grated Parmesan cheese

method
1. Cook pasta in boiling water in a saucepan following packet directions. Drain, set aside and keep warm.
2. To make sauce, heat oil in a saucepan and cook onion and garlic over a medium heat for 3-4 minutes or until onion is soft. Add tomatoes, stock, tomato purée, basil, parsley and sugar and simmer for 10-15 minutes or until reduced and thickened. Season to taste with black pepper. Spoon sauce over pasta. Sprinkle with a little grated fresh Parmesan cheese and extra chopped fresh basil.

Serves 2

tip from the chef

Any leftover sauce can be made into soup. To make, chop 1 small carrot and 1 stalk celery. Place leftover sauce, 250 ml/8 fl oz chicken stock, carrot and celery in a saucepan. Bring to simmering and simmer for 10-15 minutes or until carrot is tender. Season to taste with black pepper.

soups, pasta and rice   > 15

16 > FAMILY MEALS

cheesy noodles

soups, pasta and rice

■ □ □ | Cooking time: 15 minutes - Preparation time: 5 minutes

method
1. Prepare noodles according to packet directions. Drain, add sour cream and black pepper to taste and toss to combine.
2. Divide noodle mixture between two heatproof serving dishes and sprinkle with cheese. Place under a preheated hot grill and cook for 3-4 minutes until cheese melts and is golden.

ingredients
- 2 x 90 g/3 oz packets quick-cooking noodles
- 4 tablespoons sour cream
- freshly ground black pepper
- 60 g/2 oz tasty cheese (mature Cheddar), grated

Serves 2

tip from the chef
Accompany with a salad made of the lettuce or lettuces of your choice, cherry tomatoes, chopped or sliced red or green peppers and chopped or sliced cucumber tossed with a French dressing. Mixtures of fresh salad greens are available from many greengrocers and supermarkets. These are an economical and easy alternative to buying a variety of lettuces and making your own salads of mixed lettuce leaves.

18 > FAMILY MEALS

spicy rice tomato and vegetables

soups, pasta and rice

■ ■ ☐ | Cooking time: 40 minutes - Preparation time: 20 minutes

method
1. Heat oil in a large saucepan. Cook onion, green pepper and chili for 3-4 minutes. Add rice, mix well and cook for 3-4 minutes.
2. Add tomatoes to the pan with stock or water. Bring to the boil and simmer for 30 minutes or until liquid is absorbed and rice is tender. Season with pepper.

Serves 4

ingredients
- 1 tablespoon olive oil
- 1 onion, sliced
- 1 green pepper, diced
- 1 red chili, seeded and finely chopped
- 3/4 cup/170 g/6 oz white rice
- 3/4 cup/170 g/6 oz quick-cooking brown rice
- 400 g/13 oz canned peeled tomatoes, undrained and roughly chopped
- 1 1/2 cups/375 ml/ 12 fl oz vegetable stock or water
- freshly ground black pepper

tip from the chef
For this recipe to be really exquisite, add a handful of peeled shrimp 5 minutes before cooking is done. Shrimp shells can be boiled in low heat to obtain an excellent broth.

potato gratin

vegetables > 21

| Cooking time: 45 minutes - Preparation time: 10 minutes

method

1. Layer potatoes, onions, chives and black pepper to taste in six lightly greased individual ovenproof dishes.
2. Place yogurt and cream in a bowl and mix to combine. Carefully pour yogurt mixture over potatoes and sprinkle with Parmesan cheese. Bake at 180°C/350°F/Gas 4 for 45 minutes or until potatoes are tender and top is golden.

Serves 6

ingredients

> 1 kg/2 lb potatoes, thinly sliced
> 2 large onions, thinly sliced
> 2 tablespoons snipped fresh chives
> freshly ground black pepper
> 1¼ cup/250 g/8 oz low fat natural yogurt
> 1 cup/250 ml/8 fl oz cream (heavy)
> 60 g/2 oz grated Parmesan cheese

tip from the chef

Instead of the cream yogurt sauce, make a bechamel with 2 tablespoons butter, 2 tablespoons flour and 400 cc/13 fl oz milk.

> FAMILY MEALS

spinach
roulade

■■■ | Cooking time: 16 minutes - Preparation time: 35 minutes

ingredients
> 250 g/8 oz frozen spinach, thawed
> 1 tablespoon plain flour
> 5 eggs, separated
> 15 g/1/2 oz butter
> 1 teaspoon ground nutmeg
> freshly ground black pepper
> 2 tablespoons Parmesan cheese

mushroom filling
> 30 g/1 oz butter
> 100 g/3 1/2 oz button mushrooms, sliced
> 3 spring onions, chopped
> 440 g/14 oz canned peeled tomatoes, drained and chopped
> 1/2 teaspoon dried oregano
> 1/2 teaspoon dried basil

method
1. Place spinach, flour, egg yolks, butter, nutmeg and black pepper to taste (a) in a food processor or blender and process until combined. Transfer to a bowl.
2. Beat egg whites until stiff peaks form, then mix 2 tablespoons of egg whites (b) into spinach mixture. Fold remaining egg whites into spinach mixture.
3. Spoon into a greased and lined Swiss roll tin (c) and bake at 200°C/400°F/Gas 6 for 12 minutes or until mixture is firm.
4. To make filling, melt butter in a frying pan and cook mushrooms over a medium heat for 1 minute. Add spring onions, tomatoes, oregano and basil and cook for 3 minutes longer.
5. Turn roulade out onto a teatowel sprinkled with Parmesan cheese and roll up. Allow to stand for 1 minute. Unroll and spread with filling. Reroll and serve immediately.

Serves 6

tip from the chef
For a complete meal, serve rice cream with maple syrup as a dessert. Mix 315 g/10 oz cooked short-grain rice with 300 ml/9 1/2 fl oz double cream, whipped, and 1 teaspoon ground cinnamon. Spoon into individual serving dishes and chill. Serve topped with maple syrup.

a

vegetables > 23

b

c

24 > FAMILY MEALS

cauliflower au gratin

■□□ | Cooking time: 30 minutes - Preparation time: 10 minutes

method

1. Steam, boil or microwave cauliflower until just tender. Drain and set aside.
2. Place milk in a saucepan and cook over a medium heat until almost boiling point. Remove pan from heat and stir in cornflour mixture. Return pan to heat and cook over a medium heat until sauce boils and thickens, stirring constantly (a).
3. Combine mustard and yogurt. Remove sauce from heat and blend in yogurt mixture. Season to taste with black pepper. Spread half the sauce over the base of an ovenproof dish. Top with cauliflower (b) and remaining sauce.
4. Combine cornflakes, cheese and butter. Sprinkle on top of cauliflower. Dust lightly with paprika and bake at 180°C/350°F/Gas 4 for 15-20 minutes or until golden brown.

Serves 4

ingredients

> 1 small cauliflower, broken into florets
> 375 ml/12 fl oz milk
> 1 1/2 tablespoons cornflour blended with 3 tablespoons water
> 1 teaspoon wholegrain mustard
> 3 tablespoons natural yogurt
> freshly ground black pepper
> 60 g/2 oz crushed cornflakes
> 3 tablespoons grated mature Cheddar
> 15 g/1/2 oz butter, melted
> paprika

tip from the chef

The ideal companion for barbecued or oven roasted chicken.

a

b

grilled cod and potatoes

■ □ □ | Cooking time: 20 minutes - Preparation time: 10 minutes

ingredients

- 3 tablespoons olive oil
- 2 tablespoons lime juice
- 1 teaspoon crushed black peppercorns
- 4 cod cutlets
- 6 potatoes, very thinly sliced
- sea salt

method

1. Preheat barbecue to a medium heat. Place 1 tablespoon oil, lime juice and black peppercorns in a bowl and mix to combine. Brush oil mixture over fish and marinate at room temperature for 10 minutes.
2. Brush potatoes with oil and sprinkle with salt. Place potatoes on lightly oiled barbecue grill and cook for 5 minutes each side or until tender and golden. Move potatoes to side of barbecue to keep warm.
3. Place fish on lightly oiled barbecue grill and cook for 3-5 minutes each side or until flesh flakes when tested with a fork. To serve, arrange potatoes attractively on serving plates and top with fish.

Serves 4

tip from the chef

Fish should be bought very fresh. When it is purchased frozen, be sure the cold storage has not been suspended; the packages need to be clean and ice-free on the inside.

fish > 27

28 > FAMILY MEALS

salmon cutlets with pineapple salsa

fish

■□□ | Cooking time: 10 minutes - Preparation time: 25 minutes

method
1. Preheat barbecue to a medium heat. Cook salmon cutlets on lightly oiled barbecue for 3-5 minutes each side or until flesh flakes when tested with a fork.
2. To make salsa, place pineapple, spring onions, chili, lemon juice and mint in a food processor or blender and process to combine. Serve at room temperature with salmon cutlets.

Serves 4

ingredients
> 4 salmon cutlets, cut 2 1/2 cm/1 in thick

pineapple salsa
> 250 g/8 oz roughly chopped fresh pineapple
> 2 spring onions, finely chopped
> 1 fresh red chili, seeded and finely chopped
> 1 tablespoon lemon juice
> 2 tablespoons finely chopped fresh mint

tip from the chef
If fresh pineapple is unavailable use canned crushed pineapple in natural juice, drained, in its place. This salsa is delicious served with any fish or barbecued chicken.

snapper fillets with lemon and coriander

Cooking time: 8 minutes - Preparation time: 5 minutes

ingredients
- 1 teaspoon chopped fresh ginger
- 1 teaspoon crushed garlic
- 2 tablespoons finely chopped coriander
- 2 tablespoons olive oil
- 1 1/2 tablespoon lemon juice
- 500 g/1 lb snapper fillets (4 portions)

method
1. Mix the first 5 ingredients together in a shallow dish. Place the fillets in the dish and turn to coat well. Cover and stand 10-15 minutes.
2. Heat the barbecue to medium/hot and oil the grill bars. Place a sheet of baking paper over the bars and make a few slashes between the grill bars to allow ventilation. Place the fish on the paper and cook for 3-4 minutes each side according to thickness. Brush with marinade during cooking. Remove to plate. Heat any remaining marinade and pour over the fish.

Serves 4

tip from the chef
Fish is cooked, if when tested with a fork, it flakes or the sections pull away. Lingfish, haddock and perch may also be used.

fish > 31

fish with italian sauce

■ □ □ | Cooking time: 20 minutes - Preparation time: 15 minutes

method

1. Brush fish cutlets with lemon juice. Place under preheated grill and cook for 4-5 minutes each side. Remove from grill and keep warm.
2. Place shallots, garlic, tomatoes, mushrooms, wine, basil, oregano and pepper to taste in a saucepan. Bring to the boil, reduce heat and simmer gently for 8-10 minutes.
3. Arrange fish cutlets on serving plates. Spoon sauce over and top with Parmesan cheese.

Serves 4

ingredients

- 4 x 150 g white fish cutlets
- 2 tablespoons lemon juice
- 6 shallots, finely chopped
- 1 clove garlic, crushed
- 400 g/13 1/2 oz canned tomatoes
- 200 g/7 oz button mushrooms, sliced
- 1/2 cup/125 ml/4 fl oz red wine
- 2 teaspoons finely chopped fresh basil
- 1/2 teaspoon dried oregano
- freshly ground black pepper
- 2 tablespoons grated Parmesan cheese

tip from the chef

For a crispy effect, combine equal parts of Parmesan chesse (finely grated) and breadcrumbs. Spread over fish and gratin under oven grill.

chicken pot pie

Cooking time: 50 minutes - Preparation time: 45 minutes

ingredients
- 60 g/2 oz butter
- 1 large onion, chopped
- 4 chicken breast fillets, cut into 2 cm/3/4 in cubes
- 2 potatoes, cut into 1 cm/1/2 in cubes
- 2 large carrots, cut into 1 cm/1/2 in cubes
- 1/4 cup/30 g/1 oz flour
- 1 cup/250 ml/8 fl oz dry white wine
- 3 cups/750 ml/1 1/4 pt chicken stock
- 1 cup/250 ml/8 fl oz cream (double)
- 2 tablespoons tomato paste (purée)

herbed scone topping
- 2 cups/250 g/8 oz self-raising flour, sifted
- 1 teaspoon dried mixed herbs
- 30 g/1 oz grated fresh Parmesan cheese
- 30 g/1 oz butter, chopped
- 1 cup/250 ml/8 fl oz milk

method
1. Melt butter in a large frying pan and cook onion, stirring, over a medium heat for 3-4 minutes or until onion is soft. Add chicken and cook, stirring, for 3 minutes longer.
2. Add potatoes and carrots and cook, stirring, for 8-10 minutes. Stir in flour, then wine, stock, cream and tomato paste (purée), and bring to simmering. Simmer for 10 minutes then transfer mixture to a casserole dish.
3. To make topping, place flour, herbs, Parmesan cheese and butter in a food processor and process to combine. With machine running, add milk and process to form a sticky dough. Turn dough onto a lightly floured surface and knead until smooth. Press dough out to 2 cm/3/4 in thick and, using a scone cutter, cut out rounds and place on top of casserole.
4. Bake at 200°C/400°F/Gas 6 for 20-25 minutes or until topping is cooked and golden, and casserole is hot.

Serves 4

tip from the chef
A delicious herb topping is an imaginative alternative to potatoes in this cobbler-style recipe. Serve with a green vegetable, such as beans, spinach or cabbage, for a complete meal.

poultry > 37

thigh steaks
in fruity mint salsa

■□□ | Cooking time: 9 minutes - Preparation time: 15 minutes

method
1. Pound thigh fillets on both sides with a meat mallet to flatten. Sprinkle with salt (if using), pepper and oregano.
2. Heat a nonstick frying pan and lightly spray with oil, place in the thigh steaks and cook for 3 minutes on each side. Remove to a heated plate and keep hot.
3. Add diced pear, banana, lemon juice, mint and chili sauce to the pan. Scrape up pan juices and stir to heat fruit.
4. Pile hot fruit salsa on top of thigh steaks. Serve immediately with mashed potatoes or rice.

ingredients
> 500 g/1 lb chicken thigh fillets
> canola oil spray
> salt, pepper to taste (optional)
> 1/2 teaspoon dried oregano
> 1 pear, peeled and diced
> 1 banana, peeled and diced
> 2 tablespoons lemon juice
> 3 tablespoons finely chopped mint
> 2 teaspoons sweet chili sauce

Serves 3-4

tip from the chef
Chicken meat goes with all condiments and sauces. Such versatility allows you to prepare anything from hearty winter meals, to this lighter spring dish.

38 > FAMILY MEALS

roast turkey

■■■ | Cooking time: 3¹/₂ hours - Preparation time: 70 minutes

ingredients
> 4 kg/8 lb turkey
> 60 g/2 oz butter, melted
> 250 ml/8 fl oz chicken stock

veal forcemeat
> 30 g/1 oz butter
> 1 onion, finely chopped
> 1 rasher bacon, chopped
> 250 g/8 oz veal mince
> 185 g/6 oz breadcrumbs
> ¹/₂ teaspoon finely grated lemon rind
> 1 tablespoon finely chopped fresh parsley
> ¹/₂ teaspoon dried sage
> pinch ground nutmeg
> freshly ground black pepper
> 1 egg, lightly beaten

chestnut stuffing
> 440 g/14 oz canned chestnut purée, sieved
> 2 cooking apples, cored, peeled and grated
> 185 g/6 oz breadcrumbs
> 1 onion, chopped
> 1 stalk celery, chopped
> 4 tablespoons chopped walnuts
> 45 g/1¹/₂ oz butter, melted
> 1 tablespoon finely chopped fresh parsley
> pinch ground nutmeg
> 1 egg, lightly beaten

method
1. To make forcemeat, melt butter in a frying pan and cook onion and bacon (a) for 4-5 minutes or until bacon is crisp. Add veal, breadcrumbs, lemon rind, parsley, sage, nutmeg, black pepper to taste and egg. Mix well to combine.
2. To make stuffing, combine chestnut purée, apples, breadcrumbs, onion, celery, walnuts, parsley, butter, black pepper to taste, nutmeg and egg.
3. Remove giblets and neck from turkey. Wipe turkey inside and out and dry well. Place stuffing in body cavity and lightly fill neck end of turkey with forcemeat (b). Secure openings with metal skewers and truss legs (c) and wings.
4. Place turkey on a roasting rack in a baking dish. Brush turkey with butter, then pour chicken stock into dish. Bake at 180°C/350°F/Gas 4 for 3-3¹/₂ hours or until tender. Baste frequently with pan juices during cooking. Set aside to stand for 20 minutes before carving.

Serves 10

tip from the chef
The Spaniards brought turkeys to Europe from North America in the 1520s. Cooks soon developed wonderful dishes for special occasions with delicious stuffings and accompaniments. Try this roast turkey for Christmas or Thanksgiving dinner.

poultry > 39

a b c

barbecued chicken and mushroom patties

poultry > 41

■ □ □ | Cooking time: 16 minutes - Preparation time: 30 minutes

method
1. Place ground chicken meat in a large bowl and add remaining ingredients (a) except oil. Mix well to combine ingredients, then knead a little with one hand to make the meat fine in texture. With wet hands, shape into 4 or 5 flat patties (b).
2. Heat barbecue or grill to medium-high. Spray grill bars or rack with a little oil and place on the patties (c). Cook for 8 minutes on each side or until cooked through. Patties are cooked when juices run clear after being pricked with a skewer.
3. Serve hot with vegetable accompaniments.

Serves 4-5

ingredients
> 500 g/1 lb ground chicken meat
> 1/2 cup dried breadcrumbs
> 1 medium onion, chopped
> 1/2 teaspoon salt
> 1/2 teaspoon pepper
> 2 tablespoons lemon juice
> 2 tablespoons chopped parsley
> 1/2 cup finely chopped mushrooms
> vegetable oil

tip from the chef
For quick preparation place onion, parsley and mushrooms in a food processor and chop together. May be cooked on flat-top barbecue, electric table grill or conventional gas or electric grill.

a

b

c

lamb
and vegetable pot

■■□ | Cooking time: 90 minutes - Preparation time: 45 minutes

ingredients
> 750 g/1½ lb leg of lamb, cut into 2 cm/¾ in cubes
> 2 tablespoons seasoned flour
> 15 g/½ oz butter
> 2 tablespoons oil
> 6 baby onions, peeled and bases left intact
> 6 baby new potatoes
> 2 cloves garlic, crushed
> 3 stalks celery, sliced
> 1 red pepper, sliced
> 2 rashers bacon, chopped
> 1 carrot, sliced
> 375 ml/12 fl oz beef stock
> 125 ml/4 fl oz red wine
> 1 tablespoon tomato purée
> 2 tablespoons finely chopped fresh rosemary
> 250 g/8 oz green beans, trimmed and cut into 2.5 cm/1 in lengths
> 1 tablespoon cornflour blended with 2 tablespoons water
> freshly ground black pepper

method
1. Toss meat in flour. Heat butter and 1 tablespoon oil in a large heavy-based saucepan and cook meat in batches (a) until brown on all sides. Remove from pan and set aside.
2. Heat remaining oil in pan and cook onions and potatoes until brown on all sides. Remove from pan and set aside. Add garlic, celery, red pepper and bacon (b) and cook for 4-5 minutes. Return meat, onions and potatoes to pan. Mix in carrot, stock, wine (c), tomato purée and rosemary. Bring to the boil, then reduce heat and simmer, covered, for 1 hour or until meat is tender. Stir in beans and cornflour mixture, season to taste with black pepper and cook for 10 minutes longer.

Serves 6

tip from the chef
A whole leg lamb can be larded with garlic and rosemary, and roasted in the oven.

a

b

c

meat > 43

44 > FAMILY MEALS

family roast

meat > 45

■■■ | Cooking time: 2½ hours - Preparation time: 60 minutes

method
1. Place beef on a wire rack set in a flameproof roasting dish or tin. Brush beef with 1 tablespoon oil and sprinkle with black pepper to taste. Bake at 210°C/420°F/Gas 7 for 1-1¼ hours for medium rare or until cooked to your liking.
2. For vegetables, place potatoes, pumpkin or parsnips and onions in a large saucepan, cover with water and bring to the boil. Reduce heat and simmer for 3 minutes, then drain. Arrange vegetables in a baking dish and brush with ¼ cup/60ml/2fl oz oil. Bake, turning once during cooking, for 45 minutes or until vegetables are tender and browned.
3. To make gravy, transfer roast to a serving platter, cover with foil and rest for 15 minutes. Stir wine or stock, mushrooms, tarragon and black pepper to taste into meat juices in roasting dish or tin and place over a medium heat. Bring to the boil, stirring to loosen sediment, then reduce heat and simmer until sauce reduces and thickens. Slice beef and serve with vegetables and gravy.

ingredients
> 1½ kg/3 lb piece fresh round beef
> 1 tablespoon olive oil
> freshly ground black pepper

roast vegetables
> 6 large potatoes, halved
> 6 pieces pumpkin or 3 parsnips, halved
> 6 onions, peeled
> ¼ cup/60 ml/2 fl oz olive oil

mushroom gravy
> 1 cup/250 ml/8 fl oz red wine or beef stock
> 60 g/2 oz button mushrooms, sliced
> ½ teaspoon dried tarragon

Serves 6-8

tip from the chef
Another alternative to the mushroom sauce is a home-made mayonnaise: beat 1 egg, add a few drops of lemon and 1 cup oil in a thin stream. Add salt and blend till it thickens.

italian
sausage and pork roll

■■□ | Cooking time: 80 minutes - Preparation time: 40 minutes

ingredients
- 500 g/1 lb lean pork mince
- 250 g/8 oz Italian sausages, casings removed
- 1 onion, chopped
- 1/2 chicken stock cube
- 2 slices white bread, crusts removed
- 2 tablespoons tomato paste (purée)
- 1 egg, lightly beaten
- freshly ground black pepper
- 250 g/8 oz ricotta cheese, drained
- 2 tablespoons chopped fresh basil
- 4 slices pancetta or bacon, chopped
- 1 red pepper, roasted and sliced
- 60 g/2 oz pepperoni sausage, chopped
- 4 black olives, sliced
- 4 canned anchovy fillets, chopped
- 2 hard-boiled eggs, quartered
- 1 tablespoon olive oil
- 2 tablespoons brown sugar
- 1 teaspoon dried fennel seeds
- 1/2 teaspoon dried rosemary

method
1. Place pork, sausage meat, onion, stock cube, bread, tomato paste (purée), egg and black pepper to taste in a food processor and process to combine. Press out meat mixture on a large piece of aluminum foil (a) to form a 20 x 30 cm/8 x 12 in rectangle.
2. Spread meat with ricotta cheese and sprinkle with basil. Top with pancetta or bacon, red pepper, pepperoni, olives, anchovies and hard-boiled eggs (b), then roll up like a Swiss roll and wrap in foil (c). Place on a baking tray and bake at 180°C/350°F/Gas 4 for 40 minutes. Remove foil and drain off juices.
3. Place unwrapped roll back on baking tray and brush with oil. Combine sugar, fennel seeds and rosemary, sprinkle over roll and bake for 40 minutes longer or until cooked.

Serves 6

tip from the chef
Of Italian origin, pancetta is a type of bacon available from the delicatessen section of your supermarket or Italian food shop.

a

b

meat > 47

c

48 > FAMILY MEALS

scotch meatballs

■■□ | Cooking time: 6 minutes - Preparation time: 40 minutes

method
1. Place mince, parsley and curry powder in a bowl and mix to combine. Divide mixture into four equal portions. Place each portion on a piece of plastic food wrap and press into a 12 cm/5 in circle.
2. Combine milk and egg in a shallow dish. Dip hard-boiled eggs into milk mixture then roll in flour to coat. Place an egg in the center of each mince circle and mould around egg to enclose (a). Dip wrapped egg in milk mixture (b), then roll in breadcrumbs to coat.
3. Heat oil in a saucepan until a cube of bread dropped in browns in 50 seconds. Deep-fry meatballs, two at a time, for 5-6 minutes or until golden. Drain on absorbent kitchen paper and cool completely. Cut in half to serve.

ingredients
> 500 g/1 lb sausage mince
> 2 tablespoons chopped fresh parsley
> 1 teaspoon curry powder
> 1/2 cup/60 ml/2 fl oz milk
> 1 egg, beaten
> 4 hard-boiled eggs, peeled
> 1/2 cup/60 g/2 oz flour
> 1 cup/125 g/4 oz dried breadcrumbs
> vegetable oil for deep-frying

Makes 8 halves

a

b

tip from the chef
It's a good idea to serve these meatballs as a snack to go with a drink. In this case, make them smaller, using quail eggs. Cooking time will be shorter.

50 > FAMILY MEALS

pork
and apple cabbage rolls

■■■ | Cooking time: 90 minutes - Preparation time: 55 minutes

ingredients
> **2 tablespoons vegetable oil**
> **1 onion, finely grated**
> **2 rashers bacon, chopped**
> **1 green apple, peeled, cored and grated**
> **1 teaspoon caraway seeds**
> **500 g/1 lb lean pork mince**
> **125 g/4 oz brown rice, cooked**
> **1 egg, lightly beaten**
> **freshly ground black pepper**
> **8 large cabbage leaves**
> **60 g/2 oz butter**
> **1¹/₂ tablespoons paprika**
> **1¹/₂ tablespoons flour**
> **1 tablespoon tomato paste (purée)**
> **¹/₂ cup/125 ml/4 fl oz red wine**
> **1¹/₂ cup/375 ml/12 fl oz chicken stock**
> **¹/₂ cup/125 g/4 oz sour cream**

tip from the chef
These rolls are also delicious when made using lamb mince instead of the pork. This recipe is a good way to use up leftover cooked rice and spinach. Silverbeet leaves can be used instead of cabbage.

method
1. Heat oil in a frying pan over a medium heat, add onion and bacon and cook, stirring, for 3-4 minutes or until onion is soft. Stir in apple and caraway seeds and cook for 2 minutes longer. Remove pan from heat and set aside to cool.
2. Place pork, rice, egg, black pepper to taste and onion mixture in a bowl and mix to combine.
3. Boil, steam or microwave cabbage leaves until soft. Refresh under cold running water, pat dry with absorbent kitchen paper and trim stalks.
4. Divide meat mixture between cabbage leaves and roll up, tucking in sides. Secure with wooden toothpicks or cocktail sticks.
5. Melt 30 g/1 oz butter in a frying pan, add rolls and cook, turning several times, until lightly browned. Transfer rolls to a shallow ovenproof dish.
6. Melt remaining butter in pan over a medium heat, stir in paprika and flour and cook for 2 minutes. Stir in tomato paste (purée), wine and stock and bring to the boil. Reduce heat and simmer, stirring, for 5 minutes. Remove pan from heat and whisk in sour cream. Pour sauce over rolls, cover and bake at 180°C/350°F/Gas 4 for 1 hour.

Serves 4

meat > 51

apple pork casserole

meat > 53

■■□ | Cooking time: 80 minutes - Preparation time: 45 minutes

method
1. Heat butter in a large frying pan and cook onions and pork over a medium heat for 5 minutes. Add apples, herbs, stock and black pepper to taste, bring to the boil, then reduce heat and simmer for 1 hour or until pork is tender. Using a slotted spoon remove pork and set aside.
2. Push liquid and solids through a sieve and return to pan with pork.
3. To make sauce, melt butter in a frying pan and cook apple over a medium heat for 2 minutes. Stir in chives and tomatoes and bring to the boil, reduce heat and simmer for 5 minutes. Pour into pan with pork and cook over a medium heat for 5 minutes longer. Just prior to serving, sprinkle with cracked black peppercorns.

Serves 4

ingredients
> 30 g/1 oz butter
> 2 onions, chopped
> 500 g/1 lb lean diced pork
> 3 large apples, peeled, cored and chopped
> 1 tablespoon dried mixed herbs
> 3 cups/750 ml/1¼ pt chicken stock
> freshly ground black pepper

apple sauce
> 30 g/1 oz butter
> 2 apples, peeled, cored and chopped
> 2 tablespoons snipped fresh chives
> 440 g/14 oz canned tomatoes, undrained and mashed
> 1 teaspoon cracked black peppercorns

tip from the chef
1 cup apple jam can be used instead of the apple sauce.

54 > FAMILY MEALS

french
vanilla ice milk base

■■□ | Cooking time: 8 minutes - Preparation time: 30 minutes

ingredients

> **4¹/₄ cups/960 ml/ 1¹/₂ pt skim milk**
> **³/₄ cup/185 g/6 oz sugar**
> **2 vanilla beans or 2 tablespoons vanilla extract**
> **2 egg yolks**

method

1. In a heavy-based saucepan, heat milk, sugar, and vanilla bean. (If you are using vanilla extract, do not add it until step 4). Stir occasionally until sugar is dissolved and the mixture is hot but not boiling.
2. Whisk egg yolks together in a bowl. Continue whisking and very slowly pour in approximately 1 cup/250 ml/8 oz of the milk mixture. When smooth, pour back into the pan.
3. Whisk constantly over low heat until the mixture thickens slightly and coats the back of a spoon (about 5 minutes). Take care that the mixture doesn't boil, or it will curdle. Draw your finger across the back of the coated spoon. If the line you make remains, the custard is done.
4. Remove vanilla bean; or, if you're using vanilla extract, add it at this stage.
5. Strain into a clean bowl and cool thoroughly.
6. Transfer to an ice cream machine and freeze according to manufacturer's instructions.

Makes approximately 4 cups/900 ml/32 fl oz

tip from the chef

This recipe produces consistently excellent flavor and texture. Experiment to find which combination of ingredients is most appealing to your palate. Vanilla beans will give a richer flavor than extract.

sweet end > 55

56 > FAMILY MEALS

french bread pudding

sweet end

■■□ | Cooking time: 70 minutes - Preparation time: 45 minutes

method

1. To make filling, place figs, dates, orange juice, brandy and cinnamon stick in a saucepan and cook over a low heat, stirring, for 15-20 minutes or until fruit is soft and mixture thick. Remove cinnamon stick.
2. To assemble pudding, place one-third of the brioche slices in the base of a greased 11 x 21 cm/4 1/2 x 8 1/2 in loaf tin. Top with half the filling. Repeat layers, ending with a layer of brioche.
3. Place eggs, milk, vanilla essence and nutmeg in a bowl and whisk to combine. Carefully pour egg mixture over brioche and fruit and set aside to stand for 5 minutes. Place tin in a baking dish with enough boiling water to come halfway up the sides of the tin and bake at 160°C/325°F/Gas 3 for 45 minutes or until firm. Stand pudding in tin for 10 minutes before turning out and serving.

Serves 6-8

ingredients

> 1 loaf brioche, sliced
> 6 eggs, lightly beaten
> 1 1/2 cups/375 ml/ 12 fl oz milk
> 1 teaspoon vanilla essence
> 1 teaspoon ground nutmeg

fruit filling

> 125 g/4 oz dried figs, chopped
> 125 g/4 oz dried dates, pitted and chopped
> 1/2 cup/125 ml/4 fl oz orange juice
> 1/3 cup/90 ml/3 fl oz brandy
> 1 cinnamon stick

tip from the chef

This tempting dessert is better eaten cut into slices and served with cream shortly after it is turned out of the tin.

featherlight scones

■■□ | Cooking time: 20 minutes - Preparation time: 35 minutes

ingredients

- 4 cups/500 g/1 lb self-raising flour, sifted
- 2 tablespoons superfine sugar
- 1/4 teaspoon salt
- 60 g/2 oz butter
- 1 cup/250 ml/8 fl oz buttermilk
- 3/4 cup/185 ml/6 fl oz water
- milk for glazing
- jam or lemon curd
- whipped cream (optional)

method

1. Place flour, sugar and salt in a bowl and mix to combine. Add chopped butter (a). Using fingertips, rub in butter until mixture resembles fine breadcrumbs. Add milk and water all at once and, using a rounded knife, mix lightly and quickly to make a soft, sticky dough.
2. Turn dough onto a lightly floured surface (b) and knead lightly until smooth. Press out to make 3 cm/1 1/4 in thick rectangle (c) and using a 5 cm/2 in scone cutter, cut out rounds.
3. Place scones, just touching, in a greased shallow 18 x 28 cm/7 x 11 in baking tin (d).
4. Brush with milk and bake at 220°C/425°F/Gas 7 for 12-15 minutes or until scones are well risen and golden. Transfer to wire racks to cool.
5. To serve, split scones and top with jam or lemon curd and cream, if desired.

Makes about 20

tip from the chef

Accompany these scones with a quick lemon sauce. Blend 1 cup cream cheese with 3 tablespoons honey, 1/2 teaspoon vanilla essence and 2 tablespoons lemon juice.

a

sweet end > 59

b

c

d

60 > FAMILY MEALS

easy
chocolate cake

a

sweet end > 61

■☐☐ | Cooking time: 45 minutes - Preparation time: 20 minutes

method
1. Place milk, butter and eggs (a) in a bowl and whisk to combine.
2. Sift together flour and cocoa powder (b) into a separate bowl. Add sugar and mix to combine. Make a well in the center of the dry ingredients and pour in milk mixture. Beat (c) for 5 minutes or until mixture is smooth.
3. Pour mixture into a greased 20 cm/8 in round cake tin (d) and bake at 180°C/350°F/Gas 4 for 40 minutes or until cooked when tested with a skewer. Stand cake in tin for 5 minutes before turning onto a wire rack to cool.
4. To make icing, sift icing sugar and cocoa powder together into a bowl. Stir in milk and mix until smooth. Spread icing over cold cake.

Makes a 20 cm/8 in round cake

ingredients
> 1 cup/250 ml/8 fl oz milk
> 125 g/4 oz butter, softened
> 2 eggs, lightly beaten
> 1 1/3 cups/170 g/ 5 1/2 oz self-raising flour
> 2/3 cup/60 g/2 oz cocoa powder
> 1 cup/220 g/7 oz caster sugar

chocolate icing
> 1 cup/155 g/5 oz icing sugar
> 2 tablespoons cocoa powder
> 2 tablespoons milk

tip from the chef
To make the cake richer, cut in two layers and fill with raspberry jam.

b

c

d

original choc-chip cookies

sweet end > 63

■□□ | Cooking time: 15 minutes - Preparation time: 25 minutes

method
1. Place butter and sugar in a bowl and beat until light and fluffy. Beat in egg.
2. Add sifted flour, baking powder, coconut, chocolate chips and hazelnuts to butter mixture and mix to combine.
3. Drop tablespoons of mixture onto greased baking trays and bake at 180°C/350°F/Gas 4 for 12-15 minutes or until cookies are golden. Transfer to wire racks to cool.

Makes 35

ingredients
> 250 g/8 oz butter, softened
> 1 cup/170 g/5 1/2 oz brown sugar
> 1 egg
> 2 cups/250 g/6 oz plain flour
> 1 1/4 teaspoons baking powder
> 45 g/1 1/2 oz desiccated coconut
> 220 g/7 oz chocolate chips
> 185 g/6 oz hazelnuts, toasted, roughly chopped

tip from the chef
Everyone's favorite biscuit, it is full of the flavor of coconut, toasted hazelnuts and a generous portion of chocolate chips!

notes

my first cookbook

table of contents

Introduction 3

A Great Start
Breakfast in Bed 10
Pancake Stacks 8
Scramblers 6

Different Drinks
Banana Smoothie 12
Hot Chocolate 14
Yogurt Fruit Whiz 16

Savory Snacks
Cheesy Corn Chips 18
Eggs in a Frame 24
Flying Saucers 22
Old-fashioned Cheese on Toast 20

Super Sandwiches
Accordion Sandwich 26
American Hot Dogs 30
Hero Sandwich 28
World's Best Hamburgers 32

Tempting Vegetables
A Big Green Salad 34
Baked Jacket Potatoes 40
Cheesy Scalloped Potatoes 36
Stir-fry Vegetables 38

Pasta & Pizza
Crazy Soup 42
Macaroni Cheese 44
Real Pizza 46

For the Family
Melting Meatballs 50
Mystery Pie 48
Tasty Tacos 52

Something Sweet
Apple Crumble 54
Apricot Spice Muffins 62
Butterfly Cakes 60
Face Biscuits 58
Ice Cream Sandwiches 56

introduction

Knowing how to cook is not only a skill for life, but can be great fun too. Being able to prepare even the simplest dish provides you with a great deal of satisfaction, and enables you to work towards being independent as you grow older. This book provides simple recipes that will help you prepare snacks, drinks and meals for yourself

my first cookbook
introduction

or for the family. Use them to make sure you get the most enjoyment out of this activity, but don't forget there are some things you need to know before you start cooking.

10 Golden Rules for Success

- Always ask an adult such as your parents or an older brother or sister, if it is okay for you to cook. Also ask them to go through the recipe with you just in case you need help with some part of it. Ask if there is something you do not understand.

- First read the recipe from start to finish to make sure that you have all the ingredients and equipment that you will need. Ingredients are always listed in order of use so you can lay them out in that order.

- Always wear an apron. This will keep your clothes clean.

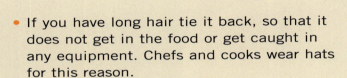

- If you have long hair tie it back, so that it does not get in the food or get caught in any equipment. Chefs and cooks wear hats for this reason.

- Wash your hands with soap and water before you start cooking. Remember to dry them well, as wet hands are slippery.

- Turn saucepans and frying pans so that the handles do not hang over the edge of the stove top.

- Take special care when plugging electrical appliances, using sharp knives and lighting the gas.

- Always use oven gloves when removing food from the oven or when handling hot saucepans or frying pans.

- Keep a clean damp cloth on hand to wipe up any spills as you go along.

- Always wash up when you have finished cooking. If something takes a while to cook this is a good time to do the washing up, otherwise do it after you have finished eating.

Difficulty scale

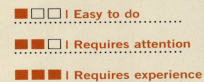

scramblers

a great start > 7

■□□ | Cooking time: 4 minutes - Preparation time: 5 minutes

method
1. Break eggs into bowl. Add milk and black pepper to taste. Whisk. Set aside.
2. Place butter in frying pan. Heat over a low heat until butter melts.
3. Add egg mixture. Cook until egg mixture is set but still creamy. Stir carefully from time to time.

ingredients
> **8 eggs**
> **2 tablespoons milk**
> **freshly ground black pepper**
> **30 g/1 oz butter**

Serves 4

junior chef says
Serve scramblers with hot toast. I like to cut a roll in half, toast it and then top with scramblers.

pancake stacks

■□□ | Cooking time: 30 minutes - Preparation time: 5 minutes

ingredients
- 1 cup/125 g/4 oz self-raising flour
- 2 tablespoons sugar
- 1 egg
- 3/4 cup/185 ml/6 fl oz milk
- 30 g/1 oz butter

junior chef says
*Top pancakes with jam, honey or golden or maple syrup. Serve with milk and muesli.
To make muesli, mix 10 chopped dried apricots, 2 cups/185 g/ 6 oz rolled oats, 1 cup/45 g/1 1/2 oz bran flakes, 4 tablespoons wheat germ, 4 tablespoons sultanas, 1/2 cup/45 g/1 1/2 oz desiccated coconut and 2 tablespoons sesame seeds.*

method
1. Place flour in sifter or sieve. Sift into large mixing bowl. Add sugar.
2. Break egg into small bowl. Add milk. Whisk.
3. Make a well in center of flour mixture. Pour in egg mixture. Beat with wooden spoon until smooth.
4. Place a little butter in frying pan. Heat over a medium-high heat until butter melts and sizzles.
5. Pour 3-4 tablespoons of batter into pan (a). Cook until bubbles form on top of pancake (b). Turn over. Cook for 1-2 minutes or until second side is brown (c).
6. Place cooked pancake on plate. Repeat with remaining batter to make 10 pancakes.
7. Stack three or four pancakes on each serving plate. Eat pancakes with your favorite topping.

Makes 10

a

b

c

a great start > 9

10 > MY FIRST COOKBOOK

breakfast in bed

a great start > 11

■ ☐ ☐ | Cooking time: 2 minutes - Preparation time: 20 minutes

method

1. To make juice, cut oranges in half. Place an orange half on squeezer. Twist to squeeze out as much juice as possible. Pour juice into glass. Repeat with remaining orange halves until you have a full glass of juice.
2. To make salad, remove green hull from strawberries. Cut strawberries in half. Peel fruit if necessary, chop, place in serving bowl. Top with strawberries. Spoon over yogurt. Drizzle with honey.
3. To make toast, place sugar and cinnamon in bowl or cup, mix. Place bread in toaster, toast until golden. Spread toast lightly with butter. Sprinkle with sugar mixture.
4. To make coffee, fill a microwave-safe mug with water. Heat on High (100%) for 1-2 minutes. Add instant coffee powder to water. Stir. Serve with or without milk and sugar.

ingredients

fresh orange juice
> 2-3 oranges

fruit salad with yogurt
> 4 strawberries
> 1-2 pieces fresh fruit of your choice
> 2 tablespoons natural yogurt
> 1 tablespoon honey

cinnamon toast
> 1 tablespoon sugar
> 1/4 teaspoon ground cinnamon
> 2 thick slices bread
> butter

a mug of coffee
> 1 cup/250 ml/8 fl oz water
> 1 teaspoon instant coffee powder

Serves 1

junior chef says

For fruit salad choose fruit that is in season. This has the best flavor and is the least expensive. In summer you could use peaches and apricots. In winter try apples and pears or bananas.

banana smoothie

Cooking time: 0 minute - Preparation time: 5 minutes

ingredients
> 1 banana
> 1/2 cup/125 ml/4 fl oz cold milk
> 1/2 cup/100 g/3 1/2 oz natural or fruit-flavored yogurt of your choice
> pinch ground nutmeg

method
1. Peel banana.
2. Place banana, milk and yogurt in food processor or blender. Process for 20-30 seconds or until thick and smooth.
3. Pour into glass. Sprinkle with nutmeg.

Makes 1

junior chef says
You can make smoothies using any fruit you like. How about trying one made with apricots, peaches or strawberries?

different drinks   > 13

hot chocolate

different drinks

■ □ □ | Cooking time: 2 minutes - Preparation time: 5 minutes

method
1. Place cocoa powder and sugar in saucepan. Slowly stir in a little milk (a) to make a smooth paste. Stir in remaining milk.
2. Boil over a low heat, stirring all the time (b).
3. Carefully pour hot chocolate into mug (c). Place marshmallow on top.

ingredients
> 1 teaspoon cocoa powder
> 1-2 teaspoons sugar, or according to taste
> 1 cup/250 ml/8 fl oz cold milk
> 1 marshmallow

Makes 1

junior chef says
It is ideal for a winter day. If you wish to give it a special flavor, add a pinch of ground cinnamon.

a

b

c

yogurt fruit whiz

■□□ | Cooking time: 0 minute - Preparation time: 5 minutes

ingredients

- 1 piece soft fruit of your choice such as a banana, peach, apricot, mango, or 125 g/4 oz strawberries or other berries of your choice
- 2 ice cubes
- 1 cup/200 g/6 1/2 oz fruit-flavored yogurt of your choice
- 1-2 tablespoons honey, or according to taste

method

1. Remove stones or pits from fruit if you need to.
2. Peel fruit if you need to.
3. Place ice cubes in plastic food bag. Wrap in newspaper. Hit several times with hammer or rolling pin to crush.
4. Place fruit, crushed ice, yogurt and honey in food processor or blender. Process until thick and smooth. Pour into glass.

Makes 1

junior chef says

If fresh fruit is not available, this drink is just as good made with canned fruit. Remember to drain canned fruit well before using.

different drinks > 17

cheesy corn chips

savory snacks > 19

■ □ □ | Cooking time: 7 minutes - Preparation time: 5 minutes

method
1. Preheat oven to 200°C/400°F/Gas 6.
2. Grate cheese (a). Set aside.
3. Cut bulb from spring onions. Remove outer leaves. Chop. Set aside.
4. Place corn chips in ovenproof dish. Sprinkle with cheese, spring onions (b) and paprika or chili powder.
5. Bake for 5 minutes or until cheese melts.

ingredients
> **60 g/2 oz tasty cheese (mature Cheddar)**
> **2 spring onions**
> **100 g/3 1/2 oz packet corn chips**
> **pinch paprika or chili powder**

Serves 2

a

b

junior chef says
If you don't have corn chips, use home bread toasts instead.

old-fashioned
cheese on toast

| Cooking time: 5 minutes - Preparation time: 5 minutes

ingredients
> **2 slices bread**
> **2 tablespoons grated tasty cheese (mature Cheddar)**
> **pinch paprika or chili powder**

method
1. Preheat grill to hot.
2. Place bread under grill. Grill for 1-2 minutes or until golden.
3. Sprinkle untoasted side of bread with cheese and paprika or chili powder.
4. Grill for 2-3 minutes or until cheese melts.

Makes 2

junior chef says

For something different try topping bread with sliced tomato or spreading with chutney, relish or jam before sprinkling with cheese. If using jam replace paprika or chili powder with ground mixed spice.

savory snacks > 21

22 > MY FIRST COOKBOOK

flying saucers

savory snacks > 23

■ ☐ ☐ | Cooking time: 5 minutes - Preparation time: 5 minutes

method
1. Preheat grill to high.
2. Cut ham or salami into strips. Set aside.
3. Cut muffin in half.
4. Spread each muffin half with tomato purée or tomato sauce.
5. Top with tomato slices. Sprinkle with ham or salami and cheese.
6. Place muffins under grill. Cook for 3-4 minutes or until cheese melts.

ingredients
> 1 slice ham or salami
> 1 wholemeal or plain muffin
> 1 tablespoon tomato purée or tomato sauce
> 2 slices tomato
> 2 tablespoons grated mozzarella cheese

Makes 2

junior chef says
See if there are any leftovers in the refrigerator you can use as a topping on your muffin. Always start by spreading your muffin with tomato purée or tomato sauce and finish by sprinkling with cheese.

24 > MY FIRST COOKBOOK

eggs in a frame

savory snacks > 25

Cooking time: 8 minutes - Preparation time: 5 minutes

method
1. Using cookie cutter cut center out of bread slices (a).
2. Place butter in frying pan. Heat over a medium heat until butter melts and sizzles.
3. Place bread in pan. Cook for 1-2 minutes or until golden. Turn over (b).
4. Break an egg into cup or small jug. Carefully pour egg into hole in one slice of bread (c). Repeat with remaining egg and bread.
5. Place lid on pan. Cook for 4-5 minutes or until eggs are cooked as you like them.

ingredients
> **2 slices bread**
> **15 g/1/2 oz butter**
> **2 eggs**

Serves 2

junior chef says
Make this recipe using your favorite type of bread. My favorite bread is wholegrain.

a

b

c

accordion sandwich

■ ☐ ☐ | Cooking time: 15 minutes - Preparation time: 10 minutes

ingredients
> 6 slices tasty cheese (mature Cheddar)
> 6 slices ham
> 1 long French breadstick
> fruit chutney or mustard, according to taste

method
1. Preheat oven to 220°C/425°F/Gas 7.
2. Line baking tray with nonstick baking paper.
3. Cut cheese slices and ham slices in half. Set aside.
4. Using serrated-edged knife, cut French breadstick into 12 even slices (a). Do not cut through base of loaf.
5. Spread one side of each cut with chutney or mustard (b).
6. Place a slice of cheese and a slice of ham in each cut.
7. Place loaf on baking tray. Bake for 10-15 minutes or until cheese just melts.

Serves 4

junior chef says
Accordion sandwich is delicious served with a big green salad (page 34).

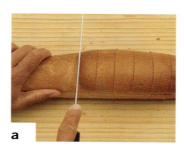

a

b

super sandwiches > 27

hero sandwich

super sandwiches

■☐☐ | Cooking time: 0 minute - Preparation time: 5 minutes

method
1. Cut French breadstick in half lengthwise. Set aside.
2. Place mayonnaise, mustard and yogurt in bowl. Mix.
3. Spread mayonnaise mixture over cut sides of breadstick. Set aside.
4. Place lettuce leaves on bottom half of breadstick. Top with ham, beef or turkey and salami.
5. Place tomatoes and cheese on top of meat. Top with other half of breadstick.
6. Tie breadstick at intervals with string. Cut into four.

Serves 4

ingredients
> 1 long French breadstick
> 4 tablespoons mayonnaise
> 1 tablespoon wholegrain mustard
> 2 tablespoons natural yogurt
> 6 large lettuce leaves
> 125 g/4 oz thinly sliced ham, roast beef or turkey
> 60 g/2 oz thinly sliced salami
> 2 thickly sliced tomatoes
> 4 slices tasty cheese (mature Cheddar)

junior chef says
To make the sandwich crunchier, melt the cheese over the bread before assembling.

american
hot dogs

| Cooking time: 5 minutes - Preparation time: 5 minutes

ingredients
> 4 long rolls
> butter
> water
> 4 frankfurters
> ketchup, mild mustard or chutney

method
1. Cut rolls in half lengthwise. Leave one side uncut. Spread lightly with butter. Set aside.
2. Three-quarters fill saucepan with water. Boil over a high heat.
3. Add frankfurters to saucepan. Boil for 5 minutes. Drain.
4. Place a frankfurter in each roll. Top with ketchup, mustard or chutney.

Makes 4

junior chef says
Serve hot dogs with a glass of juice or milk and a piece of fresh fruit and you'll have a complete meal.

super sandwiches > 31

world's best hamburgers

super sandwiches > 33

■□□ | Cooking time: 10 minutes - Preparation time: 10 minutes

method

1. To make patties, place egg and ketchup in bowl. Whisk.
2. Place bread in food processor or blender. Process to make breadcrumbs.
3. Add breadcrumbs and mince to bowl with egg mixture. Add black pepper to taste. Mix. Shape beef mixture into 6 patties (a).
4. Place vegetable oil in frying pan. Heat over a medium heat until hot. Add patties to pan. Cook for 4-5 minutes (b). Turn over. Cook for 4-5 minutes.
5. Cut rolls in half. Cut each tomato into 6 slices. Set aside.
6. To assemble burgers, place a lettuce leaf on bottom half of each roll. Top with a patty, a slice of cheese (c), 2 tomato slices, some ketchup and top of roll.

Makes 6

ingredients

> 1 tablespoon vegetable oil
> 6 white or brown round rolls
> 2 large tomatoes
> 6 large lettuce leaves
> 6 slices of your favorite cheese
> 3 tablespoons ketchup

hamburger patties

> 1 egg
> 1 tablespoon ketchup
> 2 slices stale bread
> 500 g/1 lb lean beef mince
> freshly ground black pepper

junior chef says

You might like to add some of the following to your hamburgers: beetroot slices, fried onion slices, a fried egg or a grilled bacon rasher.

a

b

c

a big green salad

■□□ | Cooking time: 0 minute - Preparation time: 10 minutes

ingredients
> 1 lettuce
> 2 stalks celery
> 1 tomato
> 1/2 cucumber
> 2 spring onions

dressing
> 2 tablespoons olive oil
> 1/4 cup/60 ml/3 fl oz lemon juice
> 1/4 cup/60 ml/3 fl oz vinegar
> 1/4 teaspoon dry mustard
> 1/2 teaspoon sugar
> freshly ground black pepper

method
1. Separate lettuce leaves. Wash in cold water. Drain in colander. Tear leaves into large pieces. Place in salad bowl.
2. Chop celery. Chop or slice tomato. Peel and slice cucumber. Cut bulbs from spring onions, remove outer leaves, chop. Add all ingredients to bowl.
3. To make dressing, place oil, lemon juice, vinegar, mustard, sugar and black pepper to taste in a screwtop jar. Place lid on jar. Shake well.
4. Pour dressing over salad. Using salad servers or two large spoons carefully toss salad.

Serves 4-6

junior chef says
Salads are great fun to make because you can add to them almost anything that you like. Try adding some of the following: sliced radishes, grated or cubed cheese, sliced raw mushrooms, sliced or grated raw carrots, chopped or sliced avocado, nuts like walnuts, almonds or peanuts and chopped fresh herbs like parsley, chives, mint and basil.

tempting vegetables > 35

cheesy scalloped potatoes

tempting vegetables > 37

■ ☐ ☐ | Cooking time: 80 minutes - Preparation time: 10 minutes

method
1. Preheat oven to 180°C/350°F/Gas 4.
2. Scrub potatoes under cold running water to remove all dirt, slice thinly (a). Peel onion, chop. Chop butter. Set aside.
3. Brush ovenproof dish with oil. Place a layer of potatoes in baking dish. Sprinkle with some onion (b) and black pepper. Top with a few pieces of butter. Repeat layers until all potato, onion and butter are used.
4. Place milk in saucepan. Stirring all the time, bring almost to boiling over a low heat.
5. Carefully pour milk over potato mixture (c).
6. Grate cheese. Sprinkle over potatoes.
7. Bake for 1-1¼ hours or until potatoes are tender.

ingredients
> **3 large potatoes**
> **1 small onion**
> **30 g/1 oz butter**
> **vegetable oil**
> **freshly ground black pepper**
> **1¼ cups/315 ml/ 10 fl oz milk**
> **60 g/2 oz tasty cheese (mature Cheddar)**

Serves 4

junior chef says
If you like garlic, finely chop one or two cloves and use them instead of onion... or along with it!

a

b

c

stir-fry vegetables

■☐☐ | Cooking time: 20 minutes - Preparation time: 10 minutes

ingredients

> 1 clove garlic
> 1 onion
> 1 carrot
> 1 small head broccoli
> 2 stalks celery
> 1 red or green pepper
> 2 spring onions
> 1 teaspoon cornflour
> 1 tablespoon soy sauce
> 1/2 cup/125 ml/4 fl oz cold stock or water
> 2 tablespoons vegetable oil
> freshly ground black pepper

method

1. Crush garlic. Peel and slice onion. Peel carrot, slice diagonally. Cut thick stems from broccoli, separate broccoli into small flowerets. Slice celery diagonally (a). Set aside.
2. Remove stems and seeds from red or green pepper, slice (b). Cut bulbs from spring onions, remove outer leaves, slice diagonally into 5 cm/2 in lengths. Set aside.
3. Place cornflour, soy sauce and stock or water in small bowl. Mix. Set aside.
4. Heat wok or frying pan over a high heat until hot. Add oil, garlic and onion. Stir-fry for 2-3 minutes.
5. Add carrot. Stir-fry for 3-4 minutes.
6. Add broccoli. Stir-fry for 3-4 minutes.
7. Add celery and red or green pepper (c). Stir-fry for 2 minutes.
8. Add cornflour mixture. Cook, stirring all the time, for 2-3 minutes or until mixture boils and thickens.
9. Add spring onions and black pepper to taste. Toss. Serve immediately.

Serves 4

junior chef says

The secret when stir-frying is to have all the ingredients prepared before you start cooking.

a

b

c

tempting vegetables > 39

baked jacket potatoes

tempting vegetables

■□□ | Cooking time: 1 hour - Preparation time: 10 minutes

method
1. Preheat oven to 200°C/400°F/Gas 6.
2. Scrub potatoes under cold running water to remove all dirt. Pierce skin of potatoes several times with fork (a).
3. Place potatoes on baking tray. Bake for 1 hour or until cooked.
4. Cut a cross in top of potatoes (b). Hold either end of each potato with clean cloth and push up (c). Set aside.
5. To make topping, cut bulb from spring onions. Remove outer leaves. Chop.
6. Top each cut potato with 1 tablespoon sour cream or yogurt. Sprinkle with 1 tablespoon cheese and some spring onions.

ingredients
> 4 medium or large potatoes —depending on how hungry you are and what else you will be having for your meal

traditional topping
> 2 spring onions
> 4 tablespoons sour cream or natural yogurt
> 4 tablespoons grated cheese

Makes 4

junior chef says
The beef mixture used in the tacos recipe (page 52) is a delicious and nutritious topping for baked potatoes.

a

b

c

crazy soup

■ □ □ | Cooking time: 35 minutes - Preparation time: 10 minutes

ingredients
- 1 onion
- 2 carrots
- 2 sticks celery
- 2 potatoes
- 440 g/14 oz canned tomatoes
- 2 tablespoons vegetable oil
- 4 cups/1 litre/1¾ pt water
- 2 chicken or beef stock cubes
- 125 g/4 oz pasta shapes
- freshly ground black pepper

method
1. Peel and chop onion. Peel and slice carrots. Trim ends from celery sticks, slice. Set aside.
2. Scrub potatoes to remove dirt. Chop. Set aside.
3. Open can. Place tomatoes and juice in small bowl. Using scissors chop tomatoes.
4. Place oil in large saucepan. Heat over a medium heat for 3-4 minutes. Add onion. Cook, stirring, for 2-3 minutes.
5. Add carrots, celery and potatoes. Cook, stirring, for 4-5 minutes.
6. Add tomatoes, water and stock cubes. Boil, stirring, for 10 minutes.
7. Add pasta shapes. Stirring, cook for 10 minutes. Add black pepper to taste.
8. To serve, ladle soup into serving bowls.

Serves 6

junior chef says

To chop tomatoes with scissors, hold the scissors upright in bowl and chop.

pasta & pizza > 43

macaroni cheese

pasta & pizza > 45

■□□ | Cooking time: 40 minutes - Preparation time: 10 minutes

method
1. Preheat oven to 200°C/400°F/Gas 6.
2. Grate cheese. Set aside.
3. Three-quarters fill large saucepan with water. Boil over a high heat. Add oil and macaroni. Boil for 10 minutes or until macaroni are cooked.
4. Meanwhile, to make sauce, place butter in medium saucepan. Heat over a medium heat until butter melts.
5. Remove from heat. Stir in flour. Return to heat. Cook, stirring, for 1 minute.
6. Remove from heat. Whisk in milk. Return to heat. Cook, stirring for 4-5 minutes or until sauce boils and thickens. Remove pan from heat.
7. Add black pepper to taste. Stir in half the grated cheese. Set aside.
8. Drain macaroni. Place in ovenproof dish. Pour sauce over. Sprinkle with remaining cheese. Sprinkle with paprika.
9. Bake for 20-25 minutes or until top is golden.

ingredients
> 125 g/4 oz tasty cheese (mature Cheddar)
> 1 teaspoon vegetable oil
> 250 g/8 oz macaroni
> 30 g/1 oz butter
> 3 tablespoons flour
> 2 cups/500 ml/16 fl oz milk
> freshly ground black pepper
> paprika

Serves 4

junior chef says
Another very traditional version consists in mixing pasta with cooked broccoli, then adding the sauce and putting it into the oven.

46 > MY FIRST COOKBOOK

real pizza

pasta & pizza > 47

■☐☐ | Cooking time: 20 minutes - Preparation time: 5 minutes

method
1. Preheat oven to 220°C/425°F/Gas 7.
2. Grate cheese. Set aside.
3. Prepare your choice of toppings —you can use just one or any combination that you like (a). Set aside.
4. Place pizza base on baking tray. Spread with tomato paste (b). Sprinkle with dried herbs (if you wish).
5. Add toppings. Sprinkle with cheese (c). Bake for 20 minutes or until base is cooked.

Serves 4

ingredients
> 90 g/3 oz mozzarella cheese
> 1 purchased pizza base
> 3 tablespoons tomato paste (purée)
> 1/2 teaspoon mixed dried herbs (if you like them)

toppings to choose
> sliced salami
> chopped ham
> tomato slices
> chopped or sliced onion
> chopped green or red pepper
> sliced or chopped green or black olives
> pineapple pieces
> sliced mushrooms
> anchovy fillets

junior chef says
Pizza is great fun to make because you can top it with whatever you like. It is also fun to arrange the food in patterns, pictures or faces.

a

b

c

mystery pie

for the family

■☐☐ | Cooking time: 50 minutes - Preparation time: 10 minutes

method
1. Preheat oven to 180°C/350°F/Gas 4.
2. Place eggs, milk and flour in large bowl. Whisk (a).
3. Open can. Drain salmon or tuna. Place in small bowl. Using fork break up. Add to egg mixture.
4. Chop red or green pepper. Grate cheese. Add both to egg mixture. Mix.
5. Add parsley (b) and black pepper to taste to egg mixture. Mix.
6. Lightly brush flan dish with vegetable oil. Pour in egg mixture (c). Bake for 45-50 minutes or until pie is firm. Stand for 5 minutes. Cut into wedges.

ingredients
- 4 eggs
- 2 cups/500 ml/16 fl oz milk
- 3/4 cup/125 g/4 oz wholemeal flour
- 100 g/3 1/2 oz canned salmon or tuna
- 1/2 red or green pepper
- 125 g/4 oz tasty cheese (mature Cheddar)
- 2 tablespoons chopped fresh parsley
- freshly ground black pepper
- 1 tablespoon vegetable oil

Serves 6

junior chef says
This is called "mystery pie" because as it cooks a crust forms on the bottom of it.

a

b

c

melting meatballs

■ □ □ | Cooking time: 30 minutes - Preparation time: 10 minutes

ingredients

> ¼ cup/60 ml/2 fl oz beef stock
> 2 eggs
> 1 teaspoon mixed dried herbs
> 1 teaspoon Worcestershire sauce
> 4 slices stale wholemeal bread
> 1 onion
> 1 carrot
> 500 g/1 lb lean beef mince
> freshly ground black pepper
> 90 g/3 oz tasty cheese
> vegetable oil
> 1 egg
> 1 cup/125 g/4 oz dried breadcrumbs
> flour

method

1. Preheat oven to 180°C/350°F/Gas 4.
2. Place stock, eggs, herbs and Worcestershire sauce in a large bowl; whisk.
3. Process bread slices, add to bowl. Peel and grate onion and carrot, add to bowl. Add beef mince and black pepper to taste, mix. Set aside.
4. Cut cheese into twelve 1 cm/¾ in cubes. Divide meat mixture into twelve equal portions. Mold one portion of meat mixture around each cube of cheese. Set aside.
5. Lightly brush baking dish with vegetable oil. Set aside.
6. Whisk egg in small bowl. Place breadcrumbs on plate. Place flour on other plate.
7. Roll each meatball in flour. Dip in egg. Roll in breadcrumbs. Place in baking dish.
8. Bake for 25-30 minutes or until cooked.

Serves 4

junior chef says

To make stock, place 1 beef stock cube and ¼ cup/60 ml/2 fl oz hot water in a bowl, mix, cool.

for the family > 51

tasty tacos

for the family > 53

■ ☐ ☐ | Cooking time: 20 minutes - Preparation time: 10 minutes

method
1. Preheat oven to 180°C/350°F/Gas 4.
2. Peel and chop onion. Crush garlic. Set aside.
3. Place oil in frying pan. Heat over a medium heat until hot. Add onion and garlic. Cook, stirring, for 5-6 minutes.
4. Add beef. Cook, stirring, for 5 minutes (a).
5. Stir in taco seasoning mix, water (b) and tomato sauce. Cook, stirring, for 5 minutes.
6. Place taco shells on baking tray. Heat in oven for 5 minutes.
7. Roll lettuce leaves, cut into strips. Cut tomatoes into small pieces. Set aside.
8. Spoon beef mixture into taco shells (c). Top with lettuce, tomato and cheese.

Serves 4

ingredients
> 1 large onion
> 2 cloves garlic (if you like it)
> 1 tablespoon vegetable oil
> 500 g/1 lb lean beef mince
> 30 g/1 oz taco seasoning mix
> 1/2 cup/125 ml/4 fl oz water
> 3 tablespoons tomato sauce
> 8 taco shells
> 4 large lettuce leaves
> 2 tomatoes
> 4 tablespoons grated tasty cheese (mature Cheddar)

junior chef says
For a complete meal serve tacos with a big green salad (page 34).

a

b

c

apple crumble

Cooking time: 35 minutes - Preparation time: 10 minutes

ingredients
> 3 apples

crumble topping
> 3/4 cup/125 g/4 oz brown sugar
> 1/2 cup/60 g/2 oz flour
> 3/4 cup/75 g/2 1/2 oz rolled oats
> 60 g/2 oz butter

method
1. Preheat oven to 180°C/350°F/Gas 4.
2. Cut apples into quarters. Cut out cores. Peel. Slice thinly.
3. Place apple slices in ovenproof dish.
4. To make topping, place sugar, flour and rolled oats in bowl. Chop butter into pieces. Add to bowl.
5. Using your fingers mix in butter until mixture is crumbly.
6. Sprinkle topping over apples. Bake for 35 minutes.

Serves 6

junior chef says
Eat it lukewarm, served with lightly whipped cream or vanilla ice-cream, and you will really enjoy it!

something sweet > 55

ice cream sandwiches

something sweet > 57

■□□ | Cooking time: 0 minute - Preparation time: 5 minutes

method
1. Spread bottom of one biscuit with ice cream.
2. Top with second biscuit.
3. Place on freezerproof dish. Freeze until ice cream is hard.

ingredients
> 2 biscuits
> 1 spoonful soft ice cream

Makes 1

junior chef says
Try these cosmic combos.
Chocolate chip biscuits with chocolate ice cream.
Chocolate chip biscuits with vanilla ice cream.
Gingernuts with vanilla ice cream.
Best of all is your favorite biscuit teamed with your favorite ice cream.

face biscuits

■ ▢ ▢ | Cooking time: 20 minutes - Preparation time: 25 minutes

ingredients
> 185 g/6 oz soft butter
> 3/4 cup/185 g/6 oz sugar
> 1 egg
> 1/4 teaspoon vanilla essence
> 1 3/4 cups/220 g/7 oz flour

vanilla icing
> 1 1/2 cup/220 g/7 oz icing sugar
> 60 g/2 oz butter, softened
> 2 tablespoons boiling water
> 1/4 teaspoon vanilla essence
> food colorings of your choice
> selection of sweets

junior chef says
If you wish to make chocolate biscuits, add 1 tablespoon cocoa powder to flour.

method
1. Beat butter and sugar in bowl until light and creamy. Add egg and vanilla essence, beat. Sift flour into mixture. Mix.
2. Turn dough onto a lightly floured surface. Knead for 3-4 minutes or until dough is smooth.
3. Divide dough into two portions. Roll each portion into a log (a). Wrap in plastic food wrap. Refrigerate for 3-4 hours.
4. Cut dough logs into 5 mm/1/4 in slices (b). Place on lined baking tray. Bake at 180°C/350°F/Gas 4 for 15-18 minutes or until biscuits are lightly browned. Place on wire rack to cool.
5. To make icing, sift icing sugar into a bowl. Add butter and boiling water, mix. Beat in vanilla essence.
6. Divide icing between small bowls. Add a few drops of food coloring to each portion of icing. Mix. Spread biscuits with icing (c). Decorate with sweets to make funny faces (d).

Makes 30

a

b

c

something sweet > 59

d

something sweet > 61

butterfly cakes

■ ■ □ | Cooking time: 15 minutes - Preparation time: 25 minutes

method
1. Preheat oven to 200°C/400°F/Gas 6.
2. Place water and butter in saucepan. Heat over a low heat until butter melts. Cool slightly.
3. Place eggs in bowl, whisk. Sift flour into bowl. Add sugar, milk and butter. Mix.
4. Spoon batter evenly into patty cake tins. Bake for 10-12 minutes or until a skewer inserted into center of a cake comes out clean.
5. Stand 5 minutes. Remove from tins. Place on wire rack to cool.
6. Cut jelly snakes into pieces. Set aside. Place cream in a bowl, whip until soft peaks form. Set aside.
7. Cut top from each cake to form a shallow hole (a). Set aside.
8. Place a little jam in each cake. Top with whipped cream (b).
9. Cut top of each cake in half (c). Place straight sides down on cream. Place a piece of jelly snake in center.
10. Place icing sugar in sifter or sieve. Sift over top of cakes.

Makes 24

ingredients
> 2 teaspoons water
> 60 g/2 oz butter
> 2 eggs
> 1 1/2 cups/185 g/6 oz self-raising flour
> 1/2 cup/100 g/3 1/2 oz caster sugar
> 1/2 cup/125 ml/4 fl oz milk

topping
> 12 jelly snakes
> 1 cup/250 ml/8 fl oz cream
> 4 tablespoons of your favorite jam
> icing sugar

junior chef says
If you want to make chocolate-flavored cakes, dissolve 2 teaspoons cocoa powder in 2 teaspoons hot water and use instead of the water.

a

b

c

apricot spice muffins

something sweet > 63

■ □ □ | Cooking time: 25 minutes - Preparation time: 10 minutes

method

1. Preheat oven to 180°C/350°F/Gas 4. Lightly brush muffin tins with vegetable oil (a).
2. Place self-raising flour, wholemeal self-raising flour and mixed spice in sifter or sieve. Sift into large bowl. Tip any husks remaining in sifter or sieve into bowl. Use scissors to cut apricots into small pieces. Add apricots to flour mixture. Set aside.
3. Place butter in saucepan. Heat over a low heat until butter melts. Pour butter into small bowl. Add lemon juice, lemon rind, sugar and egg. Whisk.
4. Pour half the butter mixture into flour mixture (b), mix. Pour in half the milk, mix. Repeat to use all the butter mixture and milk.
5. Spoon mixture into muffin tins (c). Bake for 20-25 minutes or until a skewer inserted into the center of a muffin comes out clean.
6. Stand muffins in tins for 5 minutes. Turn onto wire rack. Cool.

Makes 12

ingredients

- **vegetable oil for brushing tins**
- **1 1/4 cups/155 g/5 oz self-raising flour**
- **3/4 cup/100 g/3 1/2 oz wholemeal self-raising flour**
- **1 teaspoon ground mixed spice**
- **155 g/5 oz dried apricots**
- **90 g/3 oz butter**
- **1 tablespoon lemon juice**
- **1 tablespoon grated lemon rind**
- **1/3 cup/60 g/2 oz brown sugar**
- **1 egg**
- **1/2 cup/125 ml/4 fl oz milk**

junior chef says

I like to make these muffins at the weekend so that we have instant snack food during the week.

a

b

c

notes

Chef express

pasta supreme

table of contents

Introduction 3

Classics
Fettuccine Pesto 14
Pasta Putanesca 10
Penne Napolitana 8
Spaghetti Bolognese.................................. 12
Tomato and Basil Pasta Bake 6

Herbs and Vegetables
Cappellini with Tomatoes 32
Fettuccine with Coriander Sauce 20
Fettuccine with Leeks 22
Forest Mushroom Pasta 30
Hot Sun-dried Tomato Pasta 24
Pasta and Vegetable Stir-fry 28
Pasta with Six Herb Sauce........................ 18
Vegetable and Chili Pasta 26
Vegetable Pasta Salad 16

Creamy
Asparagus Fettuccine 34
Farfalle with Whisky Sauce 42
Fettuccine Carbonara 38
Fettuccine with Bacon and Cream 36
Gnocchi with Gorgonzola Sauce 40

Seafood
Lobster in Pasta Nets................................ 50
Quick Fettuccine with Scallops 46
Raspberry Salmon Pasta 44
Scallop and Pepper Pasta 54
Tagliatelle with Chili Octopus.................... 52
Tuna-filled Shells 48

Filled
Ravioli with Lemon Sauce 60
Ravioli with Walnut Sauce 62
Tortellini with Avocado Cream 58
Tortellini with Onion Confit 56

introduction

Due to its neutral flavour, pasta always acquires the identity of the sauce on it. Without denying the fact that a good dish of hot spaghetti, dressed with extra virgin olive oil, a bit of butter, salt and pepper can be sublime in its simplicity, in this book we propose different sauces that adapt to the

pasta supreme
introduction

shape and characteristics of each type of pasta. Since the shape defines the sauce that goes best with it, it is advisable to go over the pasta varieties available to the cook.

- **Penne or penne rigatti** (feathers, plain or striped), and in general all types of tube-shaped pasta, go well with abundant vegetable-based sauces, as they have little absorption surface.
- **Farfalle** (bows or butterflies), dried **gnocchi**, **shells**, due to their shape and size are fit to hold sauces with minced meat or juicy vegetables like tomatoes or zucchini.
- **Spaghetti, spaghettini, linguine, bucatini,** due to their firm consistency, combine well with shellfish, carbonara or Bolognese sauces, as well as with pesto.
- **Gnocchi** are suitable for creamy sauces and strong cheeses (gorgonzola, roquefort, camembert).

- **Fettuce, fettucine, tagliatelle, pappardelle, nests and all strings** are best with creamy sauces, white sauce and fish.
- **Tortellini, tortelli, cappelletti**, and in general **all filled pasta**, need lighter sauces, that combine with the filling.
- **Lasagna**, filled and baked layers of pasta, require fairly liquid sauces that can be absorbed by the dough as it cooks.
- **Angel hair** can be used for stir-fries in a wok or for other Oriental specialties.

Pasta leftovers

- They can be mixed with white sauce, sprinkled with cheese and heated under the oven grill.
- Another option is to use them to make a Spanish omelette.
- Combined with avocados, cherry tomatoes, shrimps, a few drops of olive oil, lemon juice, salt and pepper, they can be turned into a delicious salad.
- Bound together with a mixture of egg and flour, they are useful for making fritters.

Difficulty scale

■□□ I Easy to do

■■□ I Requires attention

■■■ I Requires experience

tomato
and basil pasta bake

classics

■ ☐ ☐ | Cooking time: 30 minutes - Preparation time: 20 minutes

method
1. Place hot pasta and 125 g/4 oz cheese in a lightly greased ovenproof dish, mix to combine and set aside.
2. Cook ham in a nonstick frying pan for 3-4 minutes. Add mushrooms and cook for 3 minutes longer. Spoon ham mixture over pasta and top with pasta sauce and basil. Combine breadcrumbs and remaining cheese. Sprinkle cheese mixture over pasta and bake at 200°C/400°F/Gas 6 for 20 minutes.

ingredients
- 500 g/1 lb pasta of your choice, cooked
- 220 g/7 oz tasty cheese (mature Cheddar), grated
- 8 slices ham, shredded
- 250 g/8 oz button mushrooms, sliced
- 750 g/1½ lb jar tomato pasta sauce
- 2 tablespoons chopped fresh basil
- 30 g/1 oz breadcrumbs, made from stale bread

Serves 4

tip from the chef
Accompany with a broccoli and cauliflower salad. To make salad, combine 2 tablespoons lemon juice, 2 teaspoons Dijon mustard, 3 tablespoons olive oil, 1 tablespoon finely chopped fresh parsley and black pepper to taste and toss with cooked broccoli and cauliflower florets.

8 > PASTA SUPREME

penne
napolitana

a

classics > 9

■☐☐ | Cooking time: 30 minutes - Preparation time: 20 minutes

method
1. Cook pasta in boiling water in a large saucepan following packet directions. Drain, set aside and keep warm.
2. To make sauce, heat oil in a saucepan over a medium heat. Add onions and garlic and cook, stirring (a), for 3 minutes or until onions are soft.
3. Stir in tomatoes, wine (b), parsley, oregano (c) and black pepper to taste, bring to simmering and simmer for 15 minutes or until sauce reduces and thickens.
4. To serve, spoon sauce over hot pasta (d) and top with shavings of Parmesan cheese.

Serves 4

ingredients
> 500 g/1 lb penne
> fresh Parmesan cheese

napolitana sauce
> 2 teaspoons olive oil
> 2 onions, chopped
> 2 cloves garlic, crushed
> 2 x 440 g/14 oz canned tomatoes, undrained and mashed
> 3/4 cup/185 ml/6 fl oz red wine
> 1 tablespoon chopped flat-leaf parsley
> 1 tablespoon chopped fresh oregano or 1/2 teaspoon dried oregano
> freshly ground black pepper

tip from the chef
Penne is a short tubular pasta similar to macaroni, but with the ends cut at an angle rather than straight. If penne are unavailable, macaroni are a suitable alternative for this recipe.

b

c

d

10 > PASTA SUPREME

pasta
putanesca

classics > 11

■☐☐ | Cooking time: 5 minutes - Preparation time: 20 minutes

method
1. Cook pasta in boiling water in a large saucepan following packet directions. Drain, set aside and keep warm.
2. To make sauce, heat oil in a saucepan over a low heat, add garlic and cook, stirring, for 2 minutes. Add tomatoes and bring to the boil, then stir in anchovies, black olives, capers, oregano and chili powder and simmer for 3 minutes longer. Spoon sauce over hot pasta, sprinkle with parsley and Parmesan cheese and serve.

Serves 6

ingredients
> 500 g/1 lb linguine or thin spaghetti

putanesca sauce
> 2 tablespoons olive oil
> 5 cloves garlic, crushed
> 4 x 440 g/14 oz canned peeled Italian plum tomatoes, drained and chopped
> 6 anchovy fillets, coarsely chopped
> 60 g/2 oz stoned black olives
> 2 tablespoons capers, drained and chopped
> 1 teaspoon dried oregano
> 1/4 teaspoon chili powder
> 1/2 bunch parsley, coarsely chopped
> 30 g/1 oz grated Parmesan cheese

tip from the chef
The reserved juice from the tomatoes can be frozen and used in a casserole or soup at a later date.

12 > PASTA SUPREME

spaghetti
bolognese

classics > 13

■□□ | Cooking time: 25 minutes - Preparation time: 20 minutes

method

1. To make sauce, heat oil in a frying pan over a medium heat. Add garlic and onion and cook, stirring (a), for 3 minutes or until onion is soft.
2. Add beef and cook, stirring (b), for 5 minutes or until meat is well browned. Stir in tomato purée (passata), wine or water (c), oregano and thyme. Bring to simmering and simmer, stirring occasionally, for 15 minutes or until sauce reduces and thickens. Season to taste with black pepper.
3. Cook pasta in boiling water in a large saucepan following packet directions. Drain well. To serve, spoon sauce over hot pasta and top with Parmesan cheese, if using.

Serves 4

ingredients

> 500 g/1 lb spaghetti
> grated Parmesan cheese (optional)

bolognese sauce

> 2 teaspoons vegetable oil
> 1 clove garlic, crushed
> 1 onion, chopped
> 500 g/1 lb beef mince
> 440 g/14 oz canned tomato purée (passata)
> 1/4 cup/60 ml/2 fl oz red wine or water
> 1 tablespoon chopped fresh oregano or 1/2 teaspoon dried oregano
> 1 tablespoon chopped fresh thyme or 1/2 teaspoon dried thyme
> freshly ground black pepper

tip from the chef

For an easy family meal serve this all-time favorite with steamed vegetables or a tossed green salad and crusty bread or rolls.

a

b

c

14 > PASTA SUPREME

fettuccine pesto

classics > 15

■□□ | Cooking time: 10 minutes - Preparation time: 10 minutes

method

1. Cook pasta in boiling water in a large saucepan following packet directions. Drain, set aside and keep warm.
2. To make pesto, place Parmesan cheese, garlic, pine nuts and basil in a food processor or blender and process to finely chop. With machine running, gradually add oil and continue processing to form a smooth paste. To serve, spoon pesto over hot pasta and toss to combine.

Serves 4

ingredients

> 500 g/1 lb fettuccine

basil pesto
> 100 g/3 1/2 oz fresh Parmesan cheese, chopped
> 2 cloves garlic, crushed
> 60 g/2 oz pine nuts
> 1 large bunch basil, leaves removed and stems discarded
> 1/4 cup/60 ml/2 fl oz olive oil

tip from the chef

Basil is one of the herbs that characterizes Italian cooking. This pesto can be made when basil is plentiful, then frozen and used as required. Treat yourself to this dish in mid-winter to remind you of balmy summer days.

vegetable pasta salad

Cooking time: 20 minutes - Preparation time: 20 minutes

ingredients
- 500 g/1 lb small pasta shapes of your choice
- 250 g/8 oz broccoli, broken into florets
- 250 g/8 oz cherry tomatoes, halved
- 6 spring onions, cut into 2.5 cm/1 in lengths
- 12 black olives

red wine dressing
- 2 tablespoons red wine vinegar
- 1/2 cup/125 ml/4fl oz olive oil
- 2 tablespoons grated fresh Parmesan cheese
- 1 clove garlic, crushed
- freshly ground black pepper

method
1. Cook pasta in boiling water in a large saucepan, following packet directions. Drain, rinse under cold running water, then drain again and set aside to cool completely.
2. Boil, steam or microwave broccoli for 2-3 minutes or until it just changes color. Refresh under cold running water. Drain, then dry on absorbent kitchen paper.
3. To make dressing, place vinegar, oil, Parmesan cheese, garlic and black pepper to taste in a screw-top jar and shake to combine.
4. Place pasta, broccoli, tomatoes, spring onions and olives in a salad bowl. Pour dressing over and toss to combine.

Serves 8

tip from the chef
All greens and vegetables go well with pasta and enhance its flavor.

herbs and vegetables > 17

pasta with six herb sauce

herbs and vegetables

■ ☐ ☐ | Cooking time: 15 minutes - Preparation time: 5 minutes

method
1. Cook pasta in boiling water in a large saucepan following packet directions. Drain, set aside and keep warm.
2. To make sauce, melt butter in a saucepan over a medium heat. Add rosemary, sage, basil, marjoram, oregano, parsley and garlic and cook, stirring, for 1 minute.
3. Stir in wine and stock, bring to simmering and simmer for 4 minutes. To serve, spoon sauce over hot pasta and toss to combine.

Serves 4

ingredients
> 500 g/1 lb pasta shapes of your choice

six herb sauce
> 30 g/1 oz butter
> 2 tablespoons chopped fresh rosemary
> 12 small fresh sage leaves
> 12 small fresh basil leaves
> 2 tablespoons fresh marjoram leaves
> 2 tablespoons fresh oregano leaves
> 2 tablespoons chopped fresh parsley
> 2 cloves garlic, chopped
> 1/4 cup/60 ml/2 fl oz white wine
> 1/4 cup/60 ml/2 fl oz vegetable stock

tip from the chef
Equally delicious as a light meal or as the first course of a dinner party, this dish must be made using fresh, not dried, herbs. However, the herbs can be changed according to what is available. If you can only get four of the herbs then just use those.

fettuccine
with coriander sauce

■□□ | Cooking time: 10 minutes - Preparation time: 10 minutes

ingredients
> 500 g/1 lb fettuccine

coriander sauce
> 2 cloves garlic, chopped
> 60 g/2 oz walnut pieces
> 60 g/2 oz coriander leaves
> 15 g/$^1/_2$ oz fresh parsley leaves
> 4 tablespoons vegetable oil
> 60 g/2 oz grated Parmesan cheese
> freshly ground black pepper

method
1. Cook fettuccine in boiling water in a large saucepan following packet directions. Drain, set aside and keep warm.
2. To make sauce, place garlic, walnuts, coriander and parsley in a food processor or blender and process to finely chop. With machine running, add oil in a steady stream. Add Parmesan cheese and black pepper to taste, and process to combine.
3. Spoon sauce over pasta and toss to combine. Serve immediately.

Serves 6

tip from the chef
If a milder flavor is preferred, replace coriander by fresh parsley.

herbs and vegetables > 21

fettuccine
with leeks

herbs and vegetables

■ ☐ ☐ | Cooking time: 25 minutes - Preparation time: 15 minutes

method
1. Cook fettuccine in boiling water in a large saucepan following packet directions. Drain, set aside and keep warm.
2. Heat butter in a large frying pan and cook leeks for 8-10 minutes or until tender. Add ham and red pepper and cook for 2-3 minutes longer. Stir in cream, bring to the boil, then reduce heat and simmer for 4-5 minutes.
3. Add fettuccine to pan and toss to combine. Season with black pepper (to taste) and serve immediately.

ingredients
- 500 g/1 lb fettuccine
- 60 g/2 oz butter
- 2 large leeks, halved and thinly sliced
- 185 g/6 oz ham, cut into strips
- 1 red pepper, cut into strips
- 1 cup/250 ml/8 fl oz thickened (double) cream
- freshly ground black pepper

Serves 4

tip from the chef
Leeks, spring onions, garlic, chives, shallots, all liliaceous plants are an excellent seasoning for pasta.

hot sun-dried tomato pasta

Cooking time: 15 minutes - Preparation time: 10 minutes

ingredients
- ½ bunch spring onions
- 250 g/1 lb bow pasta
- 1 teaspoon butter
- 1 tablespoon olive oil
- 1 small chili, seeded and sliced
- 2 tablespoons brandy
- 300 ml/10 fl oz cream
- ⅓ cup sun-dried tomatoes
- freshly ground black pepper

method
1. Wash and trim spring onions. Slice into 2 cm/¾ in lengths. Place pasta in boiling water and cook until al dente. Drain, and place in warm serving bowl.
2. Heat butter and oil in frying pan, sauté onions and chili for 1 minute. Add brandy, cream and sliced sun-dried tomatoes. Simmer until sauce thickens. Season with pepper.
3. Pour over pasta. Serve with Parmesan cheese and sprinkle with freshly ground black pepper to taste.

Serves 4

tip from the chef
Brandy can be replaced by a late harvest white wine, like the French Sauternes.

herbs and vegetables > 25

26 > PASTA SUPREME

vegetable
and chili pasta

a   b

herbs and vegetables > 27

■ □ □ | Cooking time: 25 minutes - Preparation time: 20 minutes

method
1. Cut eggplant into 2 cm/3/4 in cubes. Place in a colander, sprinkle with salt and set aside to drain for 10 minutes. Rinse eggplant under cold running water and pat dry.
2. Cook pasta in boiling water in a large saucepan, following packet directions. Drain, set aside and keep warm.
3. Heat oil in a large frying pan over a medium heat and cook eggplant (a) in batches, for 5 minutes or until golden. Remove eggplant from pan, drain on absorbent kitchen paper and set aside.
4. Add onions, chilies and garlic to pan and cook, stirring (b), for 3 minutes or until onions are golden. Return eggplant to pan (c). Stir in tomatoes, wine (d) and basil, bring to a simmer and cook for 5 minutes (e). To serve, spoon sauce over hot pasta.

Serves 4

ingredients
> 2 eggplant
> salt
> 500 g/1 lb pasta shells
> 1/4 cup/60 ml/2 fl oz olive oil
> 2 onions, chopped
> 2 fresh red chilies, seeded and chopped
> 2 cloves garlic, crushed
> 2 x 440 g/14 oz canned tomatoes, undrained and mashed
> 1/2 cup/125 ml/4 fl oz dry white wine
> 2 tablespoons chopped fresh basil or 1 teaspoon dried basil

tip from the chef
The combination of eggplant, tomato and goat cheese is a good flavoring for pasta.

c

d

e

pasta and vegetable stir-fry

■□□ | Cooking time: 16 minutes - Preparation time: 30 minutes

ingredients

- 30 g/1 oz dried Chinese mushrooms
- 315 g/10 oz large fusilli pasta (spirals or twists)
- 3 tablespoons vegetable oil
- 60 g/2 oz raw cashews
- 2 cloves garlic, crushed
- 1 teaspoon finely grated fresh ginger
- 315 g/10 oz Chinese cabbage, sliced
- 90 g/3 oz snow peas
- 6 spring onions, sliced diagonally
- 3 tablespoons Chinese rice wine
- 2 tablespoons light soy sauce
- 1 tablespoon sweet chili sauce

method

1. Place mushrooms in a bowl, cover with boiling water and soak for 10 minutes or until mushrooms are tender. Drain, remove stems and cut mushrooms into thin strips.
2. Cook pasta in boiling water in a large saucepan, following packet directions. Drain, set aside and keep warm.
3. Heat 1 tablespoon oil in a wok over a medium heat, add cashews and stir-fry for 1-2 minutes or until golden. Remove from pan and drain on absorbent kitchen paper.
4. Heat remaining oil in pan, add garlic and ginger and stir-fry for 1 minute. Add cabbage, snow peas, spring onions and mushrooms and stir-fry for 2-3 minutes or until vegetables change color. Stir in rice wine, soy sauce and chili sauce, bring to simmering and simmer for 1 minute. Add cashews and pasta and toss to combine.

....
Serves 4

tip from the chef

Look for Chinese mushrooms at Oriental food stores and at greengrocers. If unavailable, substitute with any fresh mushroom of your choice, or use a combination of mushrooms.

herbs and vegetables > 29

30 > PASTA SUPREME

forest mushroom pasta

herbs and vegetables > 31

■□□ | Cooking time: 20 minutes - Preparation time: 10 minutes

method
1. Cook pasta in boiling water in a large saucepan following packet directions. Drain, set aside and keep warm.
2. To make sauce, melt butter in a saucepan over a medium heat. Stir in flour and cook, stirring, for 1 minute. Remove pan from heat and whisk in milk. Return pan to heat and cook, stirring, until sauce boils and thickens. Stir in nutmeg and season to taste with black pepper. Add sauce to pasta and mix to combine. Set aside and keep warm.
3. Heat oil in a frying pan over a medium heat. Add garlic and mushrooms and cook, stirring, for 4 minutes or until mushrooms are soft. To serve, top pasta with mushroom mixture.

ingredients
> 375 g/12 oz pasta of your choice
> 2 teaspoons vegetable oil
> 1 clove garlic, crushed
> 750 g/1 1/2 lb mixed mushrooms

white sauce
> 30 g/1 oz butter
> 2 tablespoons flour
> 2 cups/500 ml/16 fl oz milk
> 1/2 teaspoon ground nutmeg
> freshly ground black pepper

Serves 4

tip from the chef
If you can only get ordinary mushrooms, add a few dried mushrooms for extra flavor. You will need to soak the dried mushrooms in boiling water for 20 minutes or until they are soft. Drain well, then slice or chop and add to the fresh mushrooms when cooking. Dried mushrooms have a strong flavor, so you only need to add a few.

cappellini with tomatoes

Cooking time: 15 minutes - Preparation time: 10 minutes

ingredients
- 120 ml/4 fl oz olive oil
- 6 cloves garlic, thinly sliced
- 550 g/17 oz Roma tomatoes, seeded and diced
- 1/3 cup fresh basil, shredded
- salt
- freshly ground black pepper
- 400 g/13 oz cappellini

method
1. Heat 60 ml/2 oz of the oil in a pan, add the garlic, and cook over a medium heat until garlic is slightly browned and golden.
2. Reduce the heat, then add the tomatoes, basil, salt and pepper, and cook for 5 minutes or until tomatoes are just heated through.
3. Cook cappellini pasta in boiling salted water until al dente. Add remaining oil.
4. Serve with tomato mixture over cappellini pasta.

Serves 4-6

tip from the chef
To peel tomatoes easily, make a small slit on the base and cover with boiling water for a few minutes. Drain, allow to cool a little and peel.

herbs and vegetables > 33

asparagus fettuccine

Cooking time: 17 minutes - Preparation time: 30 minutes

method
1. Cook pasta in boiling water in a large saucepan following packet directions. Drain, set aside and keep warm.
2. To make sauce, melt butter in a saucepan over a medium heat, add spring onions and garlic and cook, stirring, for 2 minutes or until onions are soft.
3. Stir in cream, bring to simmering and simmer for 3 minutes. Stir in asparagus and cook for 2 minutes longer. Add pine nuts and black pepper to taste. Spoon sauce over pasta and toss to combine. Serve immediately.

Serves 4

ingredients
> 500 g/1 lb fresh fettuccine

creamy asparagus sauce
> 15 g/½ oz butter
> 6 spring onions, sliced
> 1 clove garlic, crushed
> 2 cups/500 ml/16 fl oz cream (double)
> 375 g/12 oz asparagus, blanched and cut into 2.5 cm/1 in pieces
> 60 g/2 oz pine nuts, toasted
> freshly ground black pepper

tip from the chef
Fresh or packaged dried pasta? Which is the best? Neither is superior – they are just different. Fresh pasta is more delicate and keeps for only a few days, while dried pasta is more stable and ideal for serving with heartier sauces and to have on hand as a store cupboard ingredient.

fettuccine carbonara

a

creamy > 37

■□□ | Cooking time: 15 minutes - Preparation time: 10 minutes

method
1. Cook pasta in boiling water in a large saucepan following packet directions. Drain, set aside and keep warm.
2. To make sauce, cook ham, prosciutto or bacon in a frying pan (a) over a medium heat for 3 minutes or until crisp.
3. Stir in stock (b) and cream (c), bring to simmering and simmer until sauce is reduced by half.
4. Remove pan from heat, whisk in eggs (d), parsley and black pepper to taste. Return pan to heat and cook, stirring, for 1 minute. Remove pan from heat, add hot pasta to sauce and toss to combine. Serve immediately.

ingredients
> 500 g/1 lb fettuccine

carbonara sauce
> 250 g/8 oz ham, prosciutto or bacon, chopped
> 1/2 cup/125 ml/4 fl oz chicken stock
> 1 cup/250 ml/8 fl oz cream (double)
> 7 eggs, lightly beaten
> 2 tablespoons chopped flat-leaf parsley
> freshly ground black pepper

Serves 6

tip from the chef
Carbonara is a succulent, classical sauce. For a lighter version, it can be made without cream, with fewer eggs and using prosciutto ham instead of bacon.

b

c

d

… PASTA SUPREME

fettuccine
with bacon and cream

■□□ | Cooking time: 12 minutes - Preparation time: 5 minutes

ingredients
- 500 g/1 lb dried fettuccine
- 4 tablespoons grated Parmesan cheese

bacon and cream sauce
- 2 rashers of bacon, trimmed and chopped
- 4 green shallots, chopped
- 1/2 cup/125 ml/4 fl oz cream
- 1/2 cup/125 ml/4 fl oz chicken stock
- 3 tablespoons chopped sun-dried tomatoes (optional)

method
1. Cook fettuccine in boiling water in a large saucepan following packet directions. Drain and set aside to keep warm.
2. To make sauce, cook bacon in a large frying pan for 4-5 minutes or until crisp. Add shallots, and cook for 1 minute longer. Stir in cream and stock, bring to the boil then reduce heat and simmer until reduced and thickened. Stir in sun-dried tomatoes and toss fettuccine in cream sauce. Sprinkle with Parmesan cheese and serve.

Serves 4

tip from the chef
A crisp salad and crusty bread is all that is needed to complete this course.

creamy > 39

40 > PASTA SUPREME

gnocchi
with gorgonzola sauce

creamy > 41

■☐☐ | Cooking time: 15 minutes - Preparation time: 10 minutes

method
1. Cook gnocchi in boiling water in a large saucepan following packet directions. Drain, set aside and keep warm.
2. To make sauce, place gorgonzola or blue cheese, milk and butter in a saucepan and cook over a low heat, stirring, for 4-5 minutes or until cheese melts. Stir in walnuts, cream and black pepper to taste, bring to simmering and simmer for 5 minutes or until sauce reduces and thickens. Spoon sauce over hot gnocchi and toss to combine.

Serves 6

ingredients
> 500 g/1 lb potato gnocchi

gorgonzola sauce
> 200 g/6 1/2 oz gorgonzola or blue cheese, crumbled
> 3/4 cup/185 ml/6 fl oz milk
> 60 g/2 oz butter
> 60 g/2 oz walnuts, toasted and chopped
> 200 ml/6 1/2 fl oz cream (double)
> freshly ground black pepper

tip from the chef
Potato gnocchi are available from specialty pasta shops. This sauce is also great with shell pasta, penne, macaroni, tortellini or farfalle.

farfalle
with whisky sauce

■ ☐ ☐ | Cooking time: 15 minutes - Preparation time: 20 minutes

ingredients
> 375 g/12 oz farfalle

whisky and peppercorn sauce
> 15 g/½ oz butter
> 125 g/4 oz button mushrooms, sliced
> 4 spring onions, sliced
> 1¼ cups/315 g/10 oz sour cream
> 2 teaspoons French mustard
> 2 teaspoons crushed green peppercorns
> ¼ cup/60 ml/2 fl oz vegetable stock
> 1 tablespoon whisky

method
1. Cook pasta in boiling water in a large saucepan following packet directions. Drain, set aside and keep warm.
2. To make sauce, melt butter in a frying pan over a medium heat, add mushrooms and spring onions and cook, stirring, for 2-3 minutes or until mushrooms are soft.
3. Stir in sour cream, mustard, peppercorns, stock and whisky, bring to simmering and simmer for 1 minute. Spoon sauce over pasta and toss gently to combine.

Serves 4

tip from the chef
Farfalle means butterflies and this is what this pretty bow-shaped pasta looks like.

 creamy > 43

44 > PASTA SUPREME

raspberry
salmon pasta

a

■ □ □ | Cooking time: 17 minutes - Preparation time: 15 minutes

method

1. To make mayonnaise, place raspberries in a food processor or blender and process until smooth. Push purée through a fine sieve and discard seeds. Add mayonnaise, mustard and lemon juice to purée, mix to combine and set aside.
2. Cook pasta in boiling water in a large saucepan, following packet directions. Drain, set aside and keep warm.
3. Heat oil in a frying or grill pan over a medium heat. Brush salmon with lemon juice (a) and sprinkle with dill. Place salmon in pan and cook for 2-3 minutes each side (b) or until flesh flakes when tested with a fork. Remove salmon from pan and cut into thick slices (c).
4. To serve, divide pasta between six serving plates. Top with salmon slices and drizzle with raspberry mayonnaise. Serve immediately.

ingredients

> 500 g/1 lb pepper or plain fettuccine
> 1 tablespoon vegetable oil
> 500 g/1 lb salmon fillet, bones and skin removed
> 2 tablespoons lemon juice
> 2 tablespoons chopped fresh dill

raspberry mayonnaise

> 200 g/6 1/2 oz raspberries
> 1 cup/250 g/8 oz mayonnaise
> 2 teaspoons wholegrain mustard
> 1 tablespoon lemon juice

Serves 6

b

c

tip from the chef

For variation, cream can be used instead of mayonnaise.

quick fettuccine with scallops

■□□ | Cooking time: 20 minutes - Preparation time: 10 minutes

ingredients
> 500 g/1 lb fettuccine

scallop sauce
> 30 g/1 oz butter
> 1 red pepper, cut into strips
> 2 spring onions, finely chopped
> 1 cup/250 ml/8 fl oz thickened cream (double)
> 500 g/1 lb scallops
> freshly ground black pepper
> 1 tablespoon finely chopped fresh parsley

method
1. Cook fettuccine in boiling water in a large saucepan, following packet directions. Drain, set aside and keep warm.
2. To make sauce, melt butter in a large frying pan and cook red pepper and spring onions for 1-2 minutes. Add cream and bring to the boil, then reduce heat and simmer for 5 minutes or until sauce reduces slightly and thickens.
3. Stir scallops into sauce and cook for 2-3 minutes or until scallops are opaque. Season to taste with black pepper. Place fettuccine in a warm serving bowl, top with sauce and sprinkle with parsley.

Serves 4

tip from the chef
When pasta with sauce is left over, it can be reconditioned by adding milk and sprinkling cheese on it, and then baking until golden.

 seafood > 47

tuna-filled shells

seafood > 49

■□□ | Cooking time: 15 minutes - Preparation time: 25 minutes

method
1. Cook 8 pasta shells in a large saucepan of boiling water until al dente. Drain, rinse under cold running water and drain again. Set aside, then repeat with remaining shells; ensure cooked shells do not overlap.
2. To make filling, place ricotta cheese and tuna in a bowl and mix to combine. Mix in red pepper, capers, chives and 2 tablespoons grated Swiss cheese, nutmeg and black pepper to taste.
3. Fill each shell with ricotta mixture, and place in a lightly greased, shallow ovenproof dish. Sprinkle with Parmesan cheese and remaining Swiss cheese. Place under a preheated grill and cook until cheese melts.

ingredients
> 16 giant pasta shells

tuna filling
> 250 g/8 oz ricotta cheese, drained
> 440 g/14 oz canned tuna in brine, drained and flaked
> 1/2 red pepper, diced
> 1 tablespoon chopped capers
> 1 teaspoon snipped fresh chives
> 4 tablespoons grated Swiss cheese
> pinch ground nutmeg
> freshly ground black pepper
> 2 tablespoons grated fresh Parmesan cheese

Makes 16

tip from the chef
This tuna mixture, without ricotta cheese, can also be used as a sauce for ravioli, agnolotti or any pasta stuffed with ricotta cheese.

PASTA SUPREME

lobster
in pasta nets

■■■ | Cooking time: 20 minutes - Preparation time: 45 minutes

ingredients
- 375 g/12 oz angel hair pasta
- 3 uncooked lobster tails, shelled and flesh cut into 4 cm/1 1/2 in pieces
- flour
- vegetable oil for deep frying

lime cream
- 1/2 cup/125 g/4 oz mayonnaise
- 1/4 cup/60 g/2 oz sour cream
- 1 tablespoon finely grated lime rind
- 1 tablespoon lime juice
- 1 tablespoon wholegrain mustard
- 2 tablespoons chopped fresh tarragon or 1 teaspoon dried tarragon

method
1. Cook pasta in boiling water in a large saucepan until almost cooked. Drain, rinse under cold running water, drain again and pat dry on absorbent kitchen paper (a). Set aside.
2. To make lime cream, place mayonnaise, sour cream, lime rind, lime juice, mustard and tarragon in a bowl and mix to combine. Set aside.
3. Dust lobster pieces with flour. Wrap a few stands of pasta around each lobster piece (b). Continue wrapping with pasta to form a net effect around lobster.
4. Heat oil in a large saucepan until a cube of bread dropped in browns in 50 seconds. Cook pasta-wrapped lobster in batches for 2-3 minutes or until golden (c). Drain on absorbent kitchen paper and serve immediately with lime cream.

Serves 4

tip from the chef
This dish is also delicious made with large uncooked prawns.

a

b

c

seafood > 51

tagliatelle
with chili octopus

seafood > 53

■■□ | Cooking time: 22 minutes - Preparation time: 15 minutes

method

1. To make marinade, place sesame oil, ginger, lime juice and chili sauce in a large bowl and mix to combine. Add octopus, toss to coat, cover and marinate in the refrigerator for 3-4 hours.
2. Cook pasta in boiling water in a large saucepan following packet directions. Drain, set aside and keep warm.
3. To make sauce, heat oil in a saucepan over a medium heat. Add spring onions and cook, stirring, for 1 minute. Stir in tomato purée (passata), bring to simmering and simmer for 4 minutes.
4. Cook octopus under a preheated hot grill for 5-7 minutes or until tender. Add octopus to sauce and toss to combine. Spoon octopus mixture over hot pasta and toss to combine.

ingredients

> 1 kg/2 lb baby octopus, cleaned
> 500 g/1 lb spinach tagliatelle

chili ginger marinade

> 1 tablespoon sesame oil
> 1 tablespoon grated fresh ginger
> 2 tablespoons lime juice
> 2 tablespoons sweet chili sauce

tomato sauce

> 2 teaspoons vegetable oil
> 3 spring onions, sliced diagonally
> 440 g/14 oz canned tomato purée (passata)

Serves 4

tip from the chef

As a main course, all this dish needs is a sauté of mixed vegetables or a tossed green salad and crusty bread or rolls. If served on its own as a starter, it will serve six. This is also delicious made with squid rings instead of octopus.

scallop and pepper pasta

■■□ | Cooking time: 30 minutes - Preparation time: 15 minutes

ingredients

- 500 g/1 lb tagliarini
- 1 tablespoon olive oil
- 500 g/1 lb scallops
- 100 g/3 1/2 oz prosciutto or lean ham, cut into thin strips
- 2 tablespoons lemon juice
- 2 tablespoons chopped fresh basil or 1 teaspoon dried basil
- freshly ground black pepper
- 1 cup/250 ml/8 fl oz chicken stock
- 1 red pepper, cut into strips
- 2 leeks, cut into strips

gremolata

- 3 cloves garlic, crushed
- 1/2 bunch flat-leaf parsley, leaves finely chopped
- 1 tablespoon finely grated lemon rind

method

1. To make gremolata, place garlic, parsley and lemon rind in a bowl and mix well to combine.
2. Cook pasta in boiling water in a large saucepan, following packet directions. Drain, set aside and keep warm.
3. Heat oil in a frying pan over a medium heat. Add scallops and prosciutto or ham and cook, stirring, for 3 minutes or until scallops just turn opaque and prosciutto or ham is crisp. Remove pan from heat, stir in lemon juice, basil and black pepper to taste and set aside.
4. Place stock in a saucepan, bring to a simmer and cook until reduced by half. Add red pepper and leeks and simmer for 3 minutes. Add pasta and scallop mixture to stock mixture. Toss to combine and top with gremolata.

Serves 4

tip from the chef

When pepper is used to season pasta, it must always be fresh, ground in a wooden pepper mill and served at once.

seafood > 55

tortellini
with onion confit

■■□ | Cooking time: 45 minutes - Preparation time: 5 minutes

method
1. To make confit, melt butter in a saucepan over a medium heat, add onions (a) and cook, stirring, for 3 minutes or until onions are soft. Stir in sugar (b) and cook for 2 minutes longer. Add thyme, wine and vinegar (c), bring to simmering and simmer, stirring frequently, for 40 minutes or until mixture reduces and thickens.
2. Place stock in a saucepan, bring to the boil and boil until reduced by half. Keep warm.
3. Cook pasta in boiling water in a large saucepan following packet directions. Drain well. Add pasta, confit, peas and tarragon to stock, bring to simmering and simmer for 2-3 minutes or until peas are just cooked.

Serves 4

ingredients
> 1½ cups/375 ml/ 12 fl oz beef stock
> 750 g/1½ lb beef or veal tortellini
> 250 g/8 oz small peas
> 2 tablespoons chopped fresh tarragon or 1 teaspoon dried tarragon

onion confit
> 30 g/1 oz butter
> 2 onions, thinly sliced
> 2 teaspoons sugar
> 1 tablespoon chopped fresh thyme or ½ teaspoon dried thyme
> 1 cup/250 ml/8 fl oz red wine
> 2 tablespoons red wine vinegar

tip from the chef
Serve this unusual pasta dish with a sauté of mixed green vegetables and crusty bread or rolls.

a

b

c

tortellini
with avocado cream

filled > 59

■□□ | Cooking time: 5 minutes - Preparation time: 10 minutes

method
1. Cook tortellini in boiling water in a large saucepan following packet directions. Drain, set aside and keep warm.
2. To make avocado cream, place avocado, cream, Parmesan cheese and lemon juice in a food processor or blender and process until smooth. Season to taste with black pepper.
3. Place tortellini in a warm serving bowl, add avocado cream and toss to combine. Serve immediately.

ingredients
> 500 g/1 lb tortellini

avocado cream
> 1/2 ripe avocado, stoned and peeled
> 1/4 cup/60 ml/2 fl oz cream (double)
> 30 g/1 oz grated fresh Parmesan cheese
> 1 teaspoon lemon juice
> freshly ground black pepper

Serves 4

tip from the chef
Avocado can be replaced by cooked, processed zucchini. The sauce should be very hot to avoid cooling down the pasta.

ravioli
with lemon sauce

■□□ | Cooking time: 10 minutes - Preparation time: 10 minutes

ingredients
- 500 g/1 lb cheese and spinach ravioli
- 30 g/1 oz slivered almonds, toasted

lemon cream sauce
- 30 g/1 oz butter
- 1 clove garlic, crushed
- 1 1/4 cups/315 ml/10 fl oz cream (double)
- 1/4 cup/60 ml/2 fl oz lemon juice
- 30 g/1 oz grated fresh Parmesan cheese
- 3 tablespoons snipped fresh chives
- 1 teaspoon finely grated lemon rind
- 2 tablespoons chopped fresh parsley
- freshly ground black pepper

method
1. Cook pasta in boiling water in a large saucepan following packet directions. Drain, set aside and keep warm.
2. To make sauce, melt butter in a frying pan over a low heat, add garlic and cook, stirring, for 1 minute. Stir in cream, lemon juice, Parmesan cheese, chives and lemon rind, bring to simmering and simmer for 2 minutes. Add parsley and black pepper to taste and cook for 1 minute longer. Spoon sauce over pasta and toss to combine. Scatter with almonds and serve.

Serves 4

tip from the chef
Equally delicious made with cheese and spinach agnolotti (crescent or half-moon shaped ravioli) or tortellini.

filled > 61

ravioli
with walnut sauce

filled > 63

■ ☐ ☐ | Cooking time: 5 minutes - Preparation time: 10 minutes

method
1. Cook ravioli in boiling water in a large saucepan following packet directions. Drain, set aside and keep warm.
2. To make sauce, place walnuts and basil in a food processor or blender and process until finely chopped. Add butter, Parmesan cheese and black pepper to taste. With machine still running, slowly add oil and cream and process until it is just combined. To serve, spoon sauce over pasta and toss.

Serves 4

ingredients
> 750 g/1 1/2 lb cheese and spinach ravioli

walnut sauce
> 200 g/6 1/2 oz walnuts
> 1/2 bunch fresh basil, leaves removed and stems discarded
> 45 g/1 1/2 oz butter, softened
> 45 g/1 1/2 oz grated Parmesan cheese
> freshly ground black pepper
> 100 ml/3 1/2 fl oz olive oil
> 155 ml/5 fl oz cream (double)

tip from the chef
Take care when making the sauce. Only process it briefly or until the ingredients are just combined once the cream is added. If you overprocess, the cream may separate and cause the sauce to curdle.

notes

Chef express

20 take minutes!

table of contents

Soups
Beggar's Soup 10
Cold Beetroot Soup 6
Soup with Meatballs 8

Salads
Chicken and Pineapple Salad 14
Salad Niçoise 16
Tofu and Broccoli Salad 12

Dips and Sandwiches
Hummus Dip 20
Open Sandwiches 22
Salmon and Egg Sandwiches 24
White Cheese Dip 18

Starters
Avocado with Seafood 28
Melon with Prosciutto 26
Rosetta Pizzas 30

Pasta
Fettuccine with Scallops 34
Linguine with Prawns 36
Vermicelli with Broccoli and Almonds 32

Fish
Fish with Brandy Sauce 40
Fish with Green Aioli 38
Salmon with Orange Butter 42

Chicken
Chicken Breasts in Curry Sauce 44
Ginger Honey Chicken Wings 46

Meat
Herbed Lamb Patties 54
Lamb Chops with Mint Pesto 50
Veal Piccata 52
Veal Scaloppini with Sage 48

Desserts
Berry Compote 62
Fruit Salad with Lemon Syrup 56
Melon with Mint Lemon Dressing 58
Pears with Berry Coulis 60

introduction

The pleasure of good eating comes from many things. Good ingredients, enjoyable company, reliable recipes —and, of course, enough time to get everything cooked and on to the table.
For many of us time is the element that's hardest to find. We all seem to be in a constant hurry these days.

take 20 minutes!
introduction

There's work, children, shopping, keeping the house in order. Often, last of all these priorities, comes the time to cook and enjoy mealtimes together.
What can be done to help? The answer: discover quick and easy ways to cook meals everyone can enjoy. That's where this book comes in.
Every recipe has been carefully timed to help you. They clock in 20 minutes or less from start to finish, and produce good "real" food that tastes delicious.
The best thing about this book is that it puts you first. The recipes will allow you to fit in all the important things in your life —family, friends and work— and still make it possible for you to bring nice meals to the table.
All with minimum fuss and in the shortest possible time.

Time saving

As so often in the kitchen, it helps to plan ahead. A well-stocked store cupboard is a great help to speed your cooking. Check your inventory of canned food as cans are highly practical for an infinite number of recipes. The same may be said for your freezer. It is useful to have frozen ground meat, vegetables, pastries, bread and cooked rice and pasta, that can be quickly reheated in the microwave.

Being organized and assembling all your ingredients and equipment before you start will save you time in cooking and cleaning up. First of all, look at the recipe and read through the method. Then, following the ingredients listing, collect and prepare the foods you will require, then you will have them to hand when you start cooking. The ingredients are always listed in their order of use. The next step is to go through the method and get out the equipment that you will need. You should also check the recipe at this stage to see if the oven will be used and, if so, turn it on to preheat.

Now, you just have to start cooking to confirm that the preparation of a meal in 20 minutes is possible and rewarding.

Difficulty scale

■□□ | Easy to do

■■□ | Requires attention

■■■ | Requires experience

6 > TAKE 20 MINUTES!

cold
beetroot soup

soups > 7

■■□ | Cooking time: 0 minute - Preparation time: 5 minutes

method
1. Make sure beets and yogurt are thoroughly chilled.
2. Purée beets with their juice and pepper in a blender or food processor until smooth. You may need to add a little water if consistency is too thick.
3. Serve with a spoonful of yogurt on top. Garnish with parsley sprig.

ingredients
> 870 g/1 3/4 lb canned baby beets, undrained
> 1 teaspoon cracked black peppercorns
> 1/4 cup natural yogurt
> parsley for garnish

Serves 4

tip from the chef
Yogurt can be replaced by cream cheese or lightly whipped cream.

soup with meatballs

soups > 9

■ ☐ ☐ | Cooking time: 15 minutes - Preparation time: 5 minutes

method
1. In a large saucepan boil wine over high heat until reduced by half. Reduce heat to medium and add stock, tomatoes, onion and tomato paste (a). Bring to the boil, reduce heat and simmer for 1 minute.
2. Roll sausage mince into small balls, place carefully into the simmering soup (b) and cook for 7 minutes.
3. Add mushrooms, pimentos and spinach (c), cook for a further 3 minutes. Serve hot.

Serves 4

ingredients
> 1 cup dry white wine
> 3½ cups chicken stock
> 1 cup canned tomatoes, chopped
> 1 onion, sliced
> 2 tablespoons tomato paste (purée)
> 350 g/11 oz sausage mince
> 100 g/3½ oz large mushrooms, sliced
> 2 pimentos, drained and cut into thin slices
> 1 cup chopped spinach

tip from the chef
This soup results even more tasty if it is served with country bread toasts.

a

b

c

10 > TAKE 20 MINUTES!

beggar's soup

soups > 11

■□□ | Cooking time: 15 minutes - Preparation time: 5 minutes

method
1. Toast bread slices on both sides and rub it with garlic.
2. Bring chicken stock to the boil, add broccoli and cook for 30 seconds.
3. Ladle soup into warmed soup bowls, place two or three pieces of garlic toast in each bowl and sprinkle with Parmesan cheese.

ingredients
> 1 French bread stick, cut into thin slices
> 1 clove garlic, halved
> 4 cups chicken stock
> 1 cup broccoli
> 1/2 cup grated Parmesan cheese

Serves 4

tip from the chef
A good idea for winter: serve soup in ramekins and place under the grill until cheese melts.

tofu
and broccoli salad

■☐☐ | Cooking time: 3 minutes - Preparation time: 5 minutes

ingredients
- 2 1/2 cups broccoli flowerets
- 200 g/6 1/2 oz tofu, cut into 2 cm/3/4 in cubes
- 1 red pepper, seeded and cut into 1 cm/1/2 in squares
- 3 tablespoons smooth peanut butter
- 1/2 cup cream
- 3 tablespoons water

method
1. Bring a large saucepan of water to the boil, add broccoli and cook for 1 minute. Remove broccoli with a slotted spoon and refresh under cold water.
2. Arrange broccoli, tofu and pepper on serving plate.
3. Heat peanut butter in a medium saucepan over low heat. Stir in half the cream until combined. Remove from heat, stir in remaining cream and water.
4. Pour sauce over salad and serve immediately.

Serves 4

tip from the chef
Tofu, also known as soy bean curd, is a soft, cheese-like food made by curdling fresh hot soy milk with a coagulant.

salads > 13

14 > TAKE 20 MINUTES!

chicken
and pineapple salad

salads > 15

■☐☐ | Cooking time: 0 minute - Preparation time: 5 minutes

method
1. Arrange watercress, chicken pieces, pineapple, walnuts and tomatoes on serving plate.
2. Pour over combined French dressing and curry powder.

Serves 4

ingredients
> 2 cups watercress sprigs
> 1 cooked chicken, bones and skin removed, meat torn into pieces
> 1 cup canned pineapple pieces, drained
> 1/2 cup walnut halves
> 1/2 cup cherry tomatoes, halved
> 1/4 cup French dressing
> 2 teaspoons mild curry powder

tip from the chef
To make French dressing, blend or process 1/3 cup vinegar, 1 egg, 1 tablespoon sugar and 1 tablespoon paprika with salt and pepper to taste. With machine running add 1 tablespoon oil.

salad niçoise

> TAKE 20 MINUTES!

■□□ | Cooking time: 0 minute - Preparation time: 15 minutes

ingredients
- 1 lettuce of your choice, leaves separated
- 500 g/1 lb fresh young broad beans, shelled
- 1 large red pepper, cut into thin strips
- marinated artichoke hearts, halved
- 250 g/8 oz cherry tomatoes
- 1 large cucumber, cut into strips
- 3 spring onions, chopped
- 12 canned anchovy fillets, drained
- 250 g/8 oz canned tuna in water, drained
- 185 g/6 oz marinated black olives
- 6 hard boiled eggs, quartered
- 1/4 cup/60 ml/2 fl oz olive oil
- freshly ground black pepper

method
1. Arrange lettuce leaves on a large serving platter or in a large salad bowl.
2. Top with beans, red pepper, artichokes, tomatoes, cucumber, spring onions, anchovy fillets, tuna, olives and eggs.
3. Drizzle with oil and season to taste with black pepper.

Serves 4-6

tip from the chef
This is an easy spring or summer dish. As the broad beans are eaten raw it must be made with very fresh young beans. It should be noted that there are many versions of this salad and that the traditional salad does not include potatoes or other cooked vegetables.

 salads > 17

18 > TAKE 20 MINUTES!

white
cheese dip

dips and sandwiches

■ □ □ | Cooking time: 5 minutes - Preparation time: 5 minutes

method
1. Melt butter in a large saucepan over moderate heat. Add ricotta cheese, feta cheese, pepper and nutmeg. Cook for 5 minutes or until cheese softens, stirring constantly.
2. Stir in lemon juice and serve immediately on a flat plate, sprinkle with chives and accompany with chunks of crusty bread.

Serves 4

ingredients
> 60 g/2 oz butter
> 200 g/6 1/2 oz ricotta cheese
> 155 g/5 oz feta cheese
> 1/4 teaspoon ground pepper
> 1/4 teaspoon ground nutmeg
> 1 tablespoon freshly squeezed lemon juice
> 1 tablespoon finely chopped chives
> crusty bread for serving

tip from the chef
Thinly sliced prosciutto is a delicious complement for this dip.

hummus dip

■□□ | Cooking time: 0 minute - Preparation time: 10 minutes

ingredients
- 2 cups canned chickpeas, drained
- 2 cloves garlic, crushed
- 1/4 cup freshly squeezed lemon juice
- 2 tablespoons olive oil
- 1/2 cup tahini
- 1/4 teaspoon paprika
- 1 tablespoon chopped parsley
- 2 tablespoons olive oil, extra
- 4 small rounds pitta bread

method
1. In a blender or food processor place chickpeas, garlic, lemon juice, olive oil and tahini. Purée until smooth.
2. Spread hummus on a flat serving plate, sprinkle paprika and parsley on top and drizzle with extra olive oil. Serve with pitta bread.

Serves 4

tip from the chef

Tahini is a sesame paste, available in health food stores.

dips and sandwiches > 21

open sandwiches

■ ☐ ☐ | Cooking time: 5 minutes - Preparation time: 15 minutes

ingredients

pimento and cheese
- 250 g/½ lb ricotta cheese
- ½ cup grated Parmesan cheese
- 1 tablespoon chopped chives
- 4 thick slices of wholemeal bread
- 4 slices of pimento, drained
- 1 red onion, thinly sliced
- parsley to garnish

chicken and avocado
- 4 slices bread
- 50 g/1¾ oz cream cheese, softened
- 4 tablespoons mayonnaise
- 2 cups cooked chicken, bones and skin removed, meat torn into pieces
- 4 slices mature Cheddar cheese
- 1 avocado, peeled, seeded and quartered
- 1 tablespoon chopped chives

method

1. To make pimento and cheese sandwiches, combine ricotta cheese, Parmesan cheese and chives in a small bowl, mix well. Spread each slice of bread with ricotta cheese mixture, top with pimento and onion rings, garnish with parsley sprigs.
2. To make chicken and avocado sandwiches, spread each slice of bread with cream cheese, then with mayonnaise. Top with some chicken and a slice of cheese and grill until cheese has melted. Remove from grill, place avocado on top and sprinkle with chives.

Serves 4 each

tip from the chef

To inhibit the avocado from going dark, it is convenient to cut it just before serving. If you need to cut it in advance, drizzle with lemon juice.

dips and sandwiches > 23

24 > TAKE 20 MINUTES!

salmon
and egg sandwiches

dips and sandwiches

■ ☐ ☐ | Cooking time: 3 minutes - Preparation time: 5 minutes

method
1. Place eggs, cream and chives in a bowl. Using a fork, mix until well combined.
2. Melt butter in a medium frying pan over moderate heat. Pour mixture into pan and cook, stirring occasionally, for 2-3 minutes or until eggs are scrambled.
3. Butter each slice of bread and lay a slice of smoked salmon on each, top with scrambled eggs.

ingredients
> 8 eggs
> 1/4 cup cream
> 1 tablespoon chopped chives
> 60 g/2 oz butter
> 4 slices bread
> butter, extra, for spreading
> 4 slices smoked salmon

Makes 4

tip from the chef
In order to obtain a creamy texture, do not overcook egg combination.

melon with prosciutto

■□□ | Cooking time: 0 minute - Preparation time: 15 minutes

ingredients
- ½ rockmelon
- 20 very thin slices of prosciutto

lemon vinaigrette
- 3 tablespoons freshly squeezed lemon juice
- 5 tablespoons olive oil
- 1 tablespoon fresh chives, chopped
- 1 teaspoon cracked black peppercorns

method
1. Peel rockmelon, remove seeds and cut into 1 cm/½ in thick wedges. Cut each wedge in half crossways.
2. Wrap each half wedge with a slice of prosciutto, then arrange decoratively on serving plate.
3. To make vinaigrette, mix together lemon juice, olive oil, chives and pepper, pour over melon.

Serves 4

tip from the chef
The flavor of the melon will become more intense if you sprinkle it with sugar before wrapping it with the prosciutto.

starters > 27

avocado with seafood

starters > 29

■☐☐ | Cooking time: 0 minute - Preparation time: 10 minutes

method
1. Cut avocados in half and remove stones. Scoop out the flesh carefully, reserving skins.
2. Blend or process avocado flesh with lemon juice, sour cream, mayonnaise and cayenne pepper; purée until smooth. Stir in prawns.
3. Spoon mixture into avocado skins. Garnish with parsley and lemon slices.

Serves 4

ingredients
- 2 ripe avocados
- 1 tablespoon freshly squeezed lemon juice
- 1/4 cup sour cream
- 3 tablespoons mayonnaise
- 1/4 teaspoon cayenne pepper
- 155 g/5 oz cooked prawns, shelled and deveined
- 1 tablespoon finely chopped parsley
- 8 lemon slices

tip from the chef
If you wish to enrich this recipe, add a touch of ketchup to the processed mixture and add sliced hearts of palm along with the shrimp.

30 > TAKE 20 MINUTES!

rosetta
pizzas

starters > 31

■□□ | Cooking time: 10 minutes - Preparation time: 5 minutes

method
1. Spread each half roll with tomato purée, top with prosciutto, then mozzarella cheese, red pepper and parsley.
2. Bake in a moderate oven for 10 minutes or until cheese melts.

Serves 4

ingredients
- 2 rosetta rolls, halved
- 3 tablespoons tomato purée
- 8 slices prosciutto
- 4 thin slices mozzarella cheese
- 2 tablespoons red pepper, seeded and finely chopped
- 2 tablespoons chopped parsley

tip from the chef
Once out of the oven, spray with olive oil and sprinkle some chopped basil to add freshness and fragrance.

vermicelli with broccoli and almonds

Cooking time: 15 minutes - Preparation time: 5 minutes

ingredients

- 2 cups broccoli flowerets
- 4 tablespoons butter
- 2 tablespoons chopped spring onions
- 2 cloves garlic, crushed
- 1 teaspoon sambal oelek (chili paste)
- 1/2 teaspoon cracked black pepper
- 1/2 cup chopped blanched almonds
- 3 tablespoons white wine
- 3 tablespoons olive oil
- 500 g/1 lb vermicelli

method

1. Blanch broccoli in a saucepan of boiling water for 2 minutes. Drain, refresh under cold water, drain again and set aside.
2. Melt butter in a large frying pan over moderate heat, add spring onions, garlic, sambal oelek, pepper and almonds, cook for 2 minutes. Add wine and oil, cook for a further 3 minutes, then add blanched broccoli and heat through.
3. Cook vermicelli in a large saucepan of boiling water until al dente, drain and toss with broccoli mixture.

Serves 4

tip from the chef

Sambal oelek is made of chilies, with no other additives such as garlic or spices for a much simpler taste.

pasta > 33

34 > TAKE 20 MINUTES!

fettuccine
with scallops

pasta > 35

■■□ | Cooking time: 15 minutes - Preparation time: 5 minutes

method
1. Bring a large saucepan of water to the boil, add fettuccine and cook until just tender.
2. Meanwhile, melt butter in a large frying pan over moderate heat. Add red pepper and spring onions, cook for 1 minute. Add cream, bring to the boil, reduce heat and simmer for 3-5 minutes or until cream begins to thicken. Add scallops and black pepper, cook until scallops are opaque, about 1 minute.
3. Drain fettuccine and pour scallop sauce over the top, sprinkle with parsley.

ingredients
> 500 g/1 lb fettuccine
> 30 g/1 oz butter
> 1 red pepper, seeded, cut into strips
> 2 tablespoons chopped spring onions
> 1 1/2 cups cream
> 500 g/1 lb scallops
> 1/2 teaspoon ground black pepper
> 1 tablespoon chopped fresh parsley

Serves 4

tip from the chef
Always take care not to overcook the scallops because they toughen easily.

linguine
with prawns

| Cooking time: 15 minutes - Preparation time: 5 minutes

ingredients
> 500 g/1 lb linguine
> 4 tablespoons butter
> 2 cloves garlic, crushed
> 1 large onion, chopped
> 3 tablespoons pitted and chopped black olives
> 2 cups canned tomatoes, undrained
> 1 teaspoon sugar
> 1 tablespoon tomato paste (purée)
> 2 teaspoons dried rosemary, chopped
> 315 g/10 oz medium uncooked prawns, shelled and deveined, tails left intact
> 1/4 cup freshly grated Parmesan cheese
> 2 tablespoons finely chopped fresh parsley

method
1. Bring a large saucepan of water to the boil, add linguine and cook until just tender, drain, set aside.
2. Melt butter in a large frying pan over moderate heat. Add garlic, onion and olives, cook for 3 minutes, stirring constantly.
3. Add tomatoes and their juice, sugar, tomato paste and rosemary, cook for a further 5 minutes. Add prawns and cook for a further 3 minutes.
4. Add linguine to the sauce and toss well. Serve with Parmesan cheese and parsley.

Serves 4

tip from the chef
If you cannot get raw prawns, use the ones that come already cooked and add to the sauce along with the pasta.

pasta > 37

38 > TAKE 20 MINUTES!

fish with green aioli

fish > 39

■□□ | Cooking time: 5 minutes - Preparation time: 10 minutes

method
1. Melt butter in a large frying pan over moderate heat, add garlic, cook for 1 minute. Add fish pieces and cook for 2 minutes each side or until cooked through.
2. Meanwhile, to make aioli, place egg yolks, parsley, basil, chives, lemon juice and garlic in a blender or food processor. While motor is operating, gradually add oil, drop by drop, until aioli reaches a suitable consistency.
3. Arrange watercress and fish pieces on a serving plate, pour aioli over the top.

Serves 4

ingredients
> 3 tablespoons butter
> 1 clove garlic, crushed
> 440 g/14 oz bream fillets, cut into 2 cm/³/₄ in squares
> 2 cups watercress sprigs

green aioli
> 3 egg yolks
> ¹/₂ cup chopped parsley
> ¹/₂ cup chopped basil
> ¹/₄ cup chopped chives
> 2 tablespoons freshly squeezed lemon juice
> 1 clove garlic, crushed
> 1 cup oil

tip from the chef
It is important not to overcook the fish, in order to not upset its texture.

fish with brandy sauce

■■□ | Cooking time: 10 minutes - Preparation time: 5 minutes

ingredients
> 1 tablespoon butter
> 4 fish fillets, 200 g/ 6 1/2 oz each
> 4 tablespoons brandy
> 2/3 cup sour cream
> 2/3 cup cream
> 3 tablespoons freshly squeezed orange juice
> 4 tablespoons chopped roasted pistachios
> shredded orange rind for garnish

method
1. Heat butter in a large frying pan over moderate heat. Add fish fillets and cook for 3 minutes each side or until just cooked. Set aside in a warm oven.
2. Add brandy, sour cream, cream and orange juice to pan, cook until sauce is reduced by half.
3. Spoon sauce over fish fillets, sprinkle pistachios on top and garnish with shredded orange rind.

Serves 4

tip from the chef
This delicate fish recipe is ideal for entertaining without spuding much time in the kitchen.

fish > 41

42 > TAKE 20 MINUTES!

salmon
with orange butter

fish > 43

■□□ | Cooking time: 10 minutes - Preparation time: 5 minutes

method
1. To make orange butter, combine butter, orange juice concentrate, rind and parsley, mix well and set aside at room temperature.
2. Melt extra butter in a medium frying pan over moderate heat. Add salmon cutlets and cook for 3 minutes each side or until cooked through.
3. Place a cutlet on each plate, top with a tablespoon of orange butter and serve immediately.

ingredients
> 125 g/4 oz butter, softened
> 1 tablespoon orange juice concentrate
> 1 tablespoon finely grated orange rind
> 2 teaspoons finely chopped parsley
> 3 tablespoons butter, extra
> 4 salmon cutlets, 150 g/5 oz each

Serves 4

tip from the chef
Serve with orange segments and, if you wish, complete with your favorite steamed vegetables.

chicken breasts in curry sauce

■■☐ | Cooking time: 15 minutes - Preparation time: 5 minutes

ingredients
> 2 tablespoons butter
> 4 boneless chicken breast fillets
> 1/2 cup coconut milk
> 1 cup cream
> 1/4 teaspoon ground coriander
> 1/2 teaspoon ground cumin
> 2 teaspoons medium curry powder
> 2 tablespoons chopped fresh basil

method
1. Cut chicken fillets in halves (a). Melt butter in a large frying pan over moderate heat, add chicken fillets and cook until golden on both sides (b), but pink inside. Transfer fillets to a baking dish and cook in a moderately low oven for 10 minutes.
2. Meanwhile, add coconut milk, cream (c), coriander, cumin and curry powder to frying pan and cook until sauce is reduced by half.
3. Arrange chicken fillets on a serving plate, pour curry sauce over the top and sprinkle with the basil.

Serves 4

tip from the chef
Coconut milk is not the liquid inside the coconut, it is made by soaking the grated flesh of a coconut in hot water or scalded milk then straining the combination.

a

b

c

chicken > 45

46 > TAKE 20 MINUTES!

ginger honey chicken wings

chicken > 47

■■□ | Cooking time: 15 minutes - Preparation time: 5 minutes

method
1. Melt butter in a large frying pan over moderate heat. Add garlic and ginger, cook for 1 minute.
2. Add chicken wings to the pan (a) and toss them in ginger mixture, cook for 3 minutes.
3. Add honey (b), Worcestershire sauce and soy sauce and cook until sauce thickens and chicken wings are cooked, about 5 minutes.
4. Add sesame seeds (c), mix well and serve immediately.

ingredients
> 3 tablespoons butter
> 1 clove garlic, crushed
> 1 tablespoon grated fresh ginger
> 16 chicken wings
> 3 tablespoons honey
> 1/4 cup Worcestershire sauce
> 3 tablespoons soy sauce
> 3 tablespoons sesame seeds

Serves 4

tip from the chef
To intensify the flavor of the sesame seeds, toast them in a frying pan at low heat for a few minutes.

a

b

c

veal scaloppini with sage

■ ■ □ | Cooking time: 10 minutes - Preparation time: 10 minutes

method
1. Lightly dust veal fillets with flour.
2. Melt butter in a large frying pan over moderate heat. Add garlic and cook for 1 minute. Add wine and cook for a further 1 minute.
3. Add sage and fillets, cook for 2 minutes each side or until just cooked. Serve immediately with blanched vegetables if desired.

ingredients
> 8 medium veal fillets
> 1/4 cup plain flour
> 3 tablespoons butter
> 2 cloves garlic, crushed
> 3 tablespoons wine
> 2 tablespoons chopped fresh sage

Serves 4

tip from the chef
To give a different flavor to this exquisite dish, substitute rosemary or thyme for sage.

lamb chops with mint pesto

■■□ | Cooking time: 10 minutes - Preparation time: 5 minutes

ingredients
- 8 lamb chops
- 2 cloves garlic, chopped
- 1/2 cup mint leaves
- 1/4 cup parsley leaves
- 1/3 cup chopped walnut halves
- 1/4 teaspoon black pepper
- 1/3 cup olive oil

method
1. Skewer each chop to hold neatly in place. Grill chops until cooked through, about 4 minutes each side.
2. Meanwhile, place garlic, mint, parsley, walnuts and pepper in a food processor and pulse until just chopped, pouring in oil in a thin stream.
3. Serve chops with mint pesto.

Serves 4

tip from the chef
Serve with baked vegetables and you will have a complete meal.

meat > 51

veal piccata

meat > 53

■☐☐ | Cooking time: 15 minutes - Preparation time: 5 minutes

method
1. Lightly flour fillets on both sides. Shake off excess.
2. Melt butter in a medium frying pan over moderate heat. When bubbling, add fillets and sauté about 2 minutes on each side. When fillets are nearly cooked, sprinkle on lemon juice. Remove scallops from pan and keep warm.
3. Add wine to pan and boil over high heat, stirring constantly until liquid is reduced to about 1/4 cup. Pour sauce over scallops.
4. Cut lemon into paper thin slices and place 3 slices on each fillet. Serve immediately.

ingredients
> 1/4 cup flour
> 8 medium veal fillets, tenderized
> 4 tablespoons butter
> 1/2 cup freshly squeezed lemon juice
> 1/2 cup dry white wine
> 1 lemon

Serves 4

tip from the chef
The cooking time should be brief for the meat to keep its juices.

herbed lamb patties

■■□ | Cooking time: 10 minutes - Preparation time: 5 minutes

ingredients
> 2 tablespoons butter
> 2 cloves garlic, crushed
> 1/4 cup finely chopped spring onions
> 750 g/1 1/2 lb minced lamb
> 1 tablespoon finely chopped fresh thyme
> 1 tablespoon finely chopped fresh rosemary
> 1 tablespoon finely chopped fresh parsley
> 1 tablespoon freshly squeezed lemon juice
> 1 tablespoon tomato paste (purée)
> 3 tablespoons breadcrumbs

method
1. Heat butter in a medium frying pan over moderate heat. Add garlic and spring onions, cook for 1 minute.
2. In a medium bowl, combine spring onions and garlic with lamb, thyme, rosemary, parsley, lemon juice, tomato paste and breadcrumbs, mix well (a).
3. Shape mixture into 12 balls (b), flatten to form patties and grill under medium heat for 3-4 minutes (c) on each side or until cooked through.

Serves 4

tip from the chef
A mixed green salad with a simple dressing will enhance the taste these aromatic patties.

a

b

c

meat > 55

56 > TAKE 20 MINUTES!

fruit salad with lemon syrup

desserts > 57

■□□ | Cooking time: 5 minutes - Preparation time: 10 minutes

method
1. Combine lemon juice, water and sugar in a saucepan, bring to a boil, stir constantly until sugar dissolves, remove from heat, refrigerate until cold.
2. Just before serving, combine fruits in a bowl. Pour syrup over fruit, add mint and coconut, mix well.

Serves 6

ingredients
> 1/4 cup lemon juice
> 1 1/2 cup water
> 1/2 cup sugar
> 2 bananas, sliced
> 1/2 pineapple, cut into chunks
> 1 small box strawberries, hulled
> 4 passion fruit
> 2 tablespoons fresh chopped mint
> 1/3 cup desiccated coconut

tip from the chef
A scoop of vanilla ice-cream is the perfect topping for this colorful salad.

melon with mint lemon dressing

Cooking time: 0 minute - Preparation time: 10 minutes

ingredients
- 1 small honeydew melon
- 3/4 cup large strawberries, hulled, cut into small strips
- 2 tablespoons chopped fresh mint
- 2 tablespoons freshly squeezed lemon juice
- 2 tablespoons freshly squeezed orange juice
- 1 tablespoon honey
- 1 tablespoon sesame seeds

method
1. Peel melon and remove seeds. Cut the flesh into 2-3 cm/3/4-1 1/4 in thin strips.
2. Arrange melon and strawberries in 4 serving glasses.
3. In a small bowl combine mint, lemon juice, orange juice, honey and sesame seeds, mix well.
4. Pour mint lemon dressing over fruit and serve.

Serves 4

tip from the chef

Sesame seeds can be replaced by roasted slivered almonds.

desserts > 59

pears
with berry coulis

desserts > 61

■□□ | Cooking time: 0 minute - Preparation time: 15 minutes

method
1. To make coulis, place blueberries, raspberries, orange juice and icing sugar in a blender or food processor (a), blend until smooth. Push mixture through a sieve (b) and discard pips. Spoon the coulis onto each serving plate.
2. Arrange pear halves and extra blueberries on the coulis.
3. Place 4 small droplets of cream on the coulis. Carefully pull a skewer through the coulis and through the center of each droplet without lifting the skewer (c).

ingredients
> ½ cup blueberries
> 1 cup raspberries
> 4 tablespoons freshly squeezed orange juice
> 2 tablespoons icing sugar
> 12 canned pear halves, drained
> ¾ cup blueberries, extra
> ¼ cup thickened cream

Serves 4

tip from the chef
This beautiful decoration is easy to achieve if coulis has the same consistency of cream.

a

b

c

berry compote

Cooking time: 10 minutes - Preparation time: 5 minutes

ingredients
- 1 cup boysenberries or blackberries
- 1 cup raspberries
- 1/4 cup red wine
- 3 tablespoons freshly squeezed lemon juice
- 3 tablespoons sugar
- 1 cup fresh strawberries, hulled and halved
- mint to garnish

method
1. Place boysenberries or blackberries, raspberries, wine, lemon juice and sugar in a small saucepan over moderate heat, simmer gently until syrup begins to boil.
2. Remove berries from pan with a slotted spoon and set aside. Boil syrup for 5 minutes.
3. Add strawberries to the poached berries and divide between 4 serving glasses.
4. Cool syrup for 5 minutes, then pour over berries. Garnish with mint.

Serves 4

tip from the chef
When out of season, this recipe can be prepared using frozen red fruits.

desserts > 63

notes

Chef
express

zesty meat

table of contents

Introduction 3

Beef and Veal
Beef Fillet Wrapped in Pastry...................... 32
Beef Tostada Cups 18
Beef with Spinach 16
Boiled Beef Dinner 6
Carpaccio with Mustard Mayonnaise 30
Carpetburgers with Caper Mayonnaise......... 26
Cashew and Chili Beef Curry...................... 10
Cocktail Meatballs 20
Perfect T-bone Steak 8
Rack of Veal on Mashed Potatoes 24
Santa Fe Grilled Beef.................................. 14
Steak and Kidney Pie 12
Super Steak Sandwiches 22
Veal Chops with Sun-dried Tomatoes 28
Wellington Bread Loaf 35

Pork
Balsamic Pork Stir-fry 48
Chili Meat Pattie Casserole........................ 52
Chinese Spareribs 44
Honey-glazed Spareribs 50
Pork with Mango Couscous 38
Pork with Mole and Dumplings 46
Roast Pork with Apple Stuffing 40
Spiced Pork Fillet 42

Lamb
Barbecued Lamb Pitta Breads 60
Chargrilled Lamb with Mint Pesto 54
Crispy Lamb Tortilla Pizza 58
Slow-baked Chili Lamb 62
Thai Lamb and Noodle Salad 56

introduction

Meats are the undisputable pillars of human nutrition. Whether beef, veal, pork or lamb, they are always part of the menu. Even when today's tendency is looking to reduce the ingestion of meats, they should not be cut out entirely, but rather prepared in a savvy, healthy way. A meal which includes some type of meat two or three times a week should not be missing from any balanced diet.

zesty meat
introduction

Making the best choice

Choosing the right meat is difficult given the variety of options on the market. Bovine, porcine or ovine meats are displayed in shop windows in diverse cuts and qualities, whose characteristics the consumer will supposedly be able to distinguish as the most suitable for different recipe requirements.

- For carpaccio, meat should be tender, very fresh and little infiltrated by fat. To get the required thin cutlets, store meat in the freezer until completely frozen. Then, it will be easy to cut in thin pieces with an electric knife or meat slicer.
- For lamb barbecues, carve the upper foreleg in thin slices.
- For grilled or barbecued steaks, meat cuts with bone are preferable.
- Racks of lamb may be cooked in one piece or cut into chops in groups of three.
- The meat for stews need not be tender. Quite the opposite, fibrous meats and less delicate cuts are the ideal.

Secrets

- There are two basic secrets for cooking meats: grilled chops or sirloin steaks should be done on a high flame, almost instantly, two to three minutes per side, so that meat may preserve its juice. On the contrary, stews should be cooked for over 50 minutes, so meat is tender and impregnated with flavor.
- Marinades are indispensable for enhancing flavors of oriental stir-fries or brochettes; in this case, the liquid can also be brushed onto meat to prevent dryness.
- Mix drops of sesame oil, olive oil, soy sauce with sesame seeds or coriander to get the perfect condiment for oriental skewers.

Difficulty scale

■□□ I Easy to do

■■□ I Requires attention

■■■ I Requires experience

> ZESTY MEAT

boiled
beef dinner

■□□ | Cooking time: 2 hours - Preparation time: 10 minutes

ingredients
- 1 1/2 kg/3 lb corned beef silverside
- 2 tablespoons brown sugar
- 1 tablespoon cider vinegar
- 2 sprigs fresh mint
- 1 onion, peeled and studded with 4 whole cloves
- 6 peppercorns
- 6 small carrots, peeled
- 6 small onions, peeled
- 3 parsnips, peeled and halved

redcurrant glaze
- 1/2 cup/155 g redcurrant jelly
- 2 tablespoons orange juice
- 1 tablespoon Grand Marnier liqueur

method
1. Place meat in a large heavy-based saucepan. Add brown sugar, vinegar, mint, onion, peppercorns and enough water to cover meat. Bring to the boil, then reduce heat and simmer for 1 1/4-1 1/2 hours.
2. Add carrots, onions and parsnips to pan and cook over a low heat for 40 minutes longer or until vegetables are tender.
3. To make glaze, place redcurrant jelly, orange juice and Grand Marnier in a small saucepan and cook over a low heat, stirring occasionally, until well blended. Transfer meat to a serving plate and brush with redcurrant mixture. Slice meat and serve with vegetables and any remaining redcurrant mixture.

Serves 6

tip from the chef
Simple and satisfying, this boiled beef dinner is served with creamy mashed potatoes and horseradish cream. There are sure to be requests for second helpings. To make horseradish cream, whip 1/2 cup/125 ml cream until soft peaks form, then fold through 3 tablespoons horseradish relish.

beef and veal > 7

8 > ZESTY MEAT

perfect
t-bone steak

beef and veal > 9

■□□ | Cooking time: 15 minutes - Preparation time: 10 minutes

method

1. Bring the steaks to room temperate. Mix garlic, oil and salt and pepper together. Rub onto both sides of the steak. Stand for 10-15 minutes at room temperature.
2. Heat the barbecue until hot and oil the grill bars. Arrange the steaks and sear for one minute each side. Move steaks to cooler part of the barbecue to continue cooking over moderate heat, or turn heat down. If heat cannot be reduced then elevate on a wire cake-rack placed on the grill bars. Cook until desired level is achieved. Total time 5-6 minutes for rare, 7-10 minutes for medium and 10-14 minutes for well done. Turn during cooking.
3. To make garlic butter, mix all ingredients together. Place steaks on a heated steak plate and top with a dollop of garlic butter; serve remaining butter in a pot with a spoon. Accompany with jacket potatoes.

ingredients

> 4 T-bone steaks
> 2 teaspoons crushed garlic
> 2 teaspoons oil
> salt and pepper

garlic butter

> 60 g/2 oz butter
> 1 teaspoon crushed garlic
> 1 tablespoon parsley flakes
> 2 teaspoons lemon juice

Serves 4

tip from the chef

Many a time this delicious steak has been ruined on the barbecue. This recipe is suitable for all barbecues, but improvise a hood if using a flat-top barbecue.

10 > ZESTY MEAT

cashew
and chili beef curry

■ ■ □ | Cooking time: 30 minutes - Preparation time: 35 minutes

ingredients

> 3 cm/1¼ in piece fresh galanga or ginger, chopped, or 5 slices bottled galanga, chopped
> 1 stalk fresh lemon grass, finely sliced, or ½ teaspoon dried lemon grass, soaked in hot water until soft
> 3 kaffir lime leaves, finely shredded
> 2 small fresh red chilies, seeded and chopped
> 2 teaspoons shrimp paste
> 2 tablespoons Thai fish sauce (nam pla)
> 1 tablespoon lime juice
> 2 tablespoons peanut oil
> 4 red or golden shallots, sliced
> 2 garlic cloves, chopped
> 3 small fresh red chillies, sliced
> 500 g/1 lb round or blade steak, cut into 2 cm/¾ in cubes
> 2 cups/500 ml/16 fl oz beef stock
> 250 g/8 oz okra, trimmed
> 60 g/2 oz cashews, roughly chopped
> 1 tablespoon palm or brown sugar
> 2 tablespoons light soy sauce

method

1. Place galanga or ginger, lemon grass, lime leaves, chopped chilies, shrimp paste, fish sauce and lime juice in a food processor and process to make a thick paste, adding a little water if necessary.
2. Heat 1 tablespoon oil in a wok or large saucepan over a medium heat, add shallots, garlic, sliced red chilies and spice paste and cook, stirring, for 2-3 minutes or until fragrant. Remove and set aside.
3. Heat remaining oil in wok over a high heat and stir-fry beef, in batches, until brown. Return spice paste to pan, stir in stock and okra and bring to the boil. Reduce heat and simmer, stirring occasionally, for 15 minutes.
4. Stir in cashews, sugar and soy sauce and simmer for 10 minutes longer or until beef is tender.

Serves 4

tip from the chef
Curries, like all stews, are tastier when prepared with the sufficient anticipation so as to be reheated before serving.

beef and veal > 11

12 > ZESTY MEAT

steak
and kidney pie

beef and veal

■■■ | Cooking time: 3 hours - Preparation time: 1 hour

method
1. Place steak, kidneys and flour in a plastic food bag and shake to coat meat with flour. Shake off excess flour and set aside. Heat oil in a large frying pan and cook meat over a high heat, stirring, until brown on all sides. Reduce heat to medium, add garlic and onions and cook for 3 minutes longer. Stir in mustard, parsley, Worcestershire sauce, stock and tomato paste (purée), bring to simmering, cover and simmer, stirring occasionally, for 2 1/2 hours or until meat is tender. Remove pan from heat and set aside to cool completely.
2. Place cooled filling in a 4 cup/1 liter/ 1 3/4 pt capacity pie dish. On a lightly floured surface, roll out pastry to 5 cm/2 in larger than pie dish. Cut off a 1 cm/1/2 in strip from pastry edge. Brush rim of dish with water and press pastry strip onto rim. Brush pastry strip with water. Lift pastry top over filling and press gently to seal edges. Trim and knock back edges to make a decorative edge. Brush with milk and bake at 210°C/420°F/Gas 7 for 30 minutes or until pastry is golden and crisp.

ingredients
> 1 kg/2 lb lean topside steak, cut into 2 1/2 cm/ 1 in cubes
> 6 lamb kidneys or 1 ox kidney, cored and roughly chopped
> 4 tablespoons flour
> 1 tablespoon vegetable oil
> 2 cloves garlic, crushed
> 1/2 teaspoon dry mustard
> 2 tablespoons chopped fresh parsley
> 2 tablespoons Worcestershire sauce
> 1 1/2 cups/375 ml/12 fl oz beef stock
> 2 teaspoons tomato paste (purée)
> 375 g/12 oz prepared puff pastry
> 2 tablespoons milk

Serves 6

tip from the chef
To lower the cholesterol content of meat, remove all the visible fat before cooking.

14 > ZESTY MEAT

santa fe
grilled beef

beef and veal   > 15

■ ☐ ☐ | Cooking time: 4 minutes - Preparation time: 15 minutes

method

1. To make spice mix, place onion, garlic, chili powder, lime rind, cumin, oil and lime juice in a bowl (a) and mix to combine.
2. Place steaks between sheets of plastic food wrap. Pound with a meat mallet or rolling pin until steaks are 5 mm/$^1/_4$ in thick. Divide spice mix into steaks (b).
3. Cook steaks on a preheated hot barbecue or in a frying pan (c) for 30-60 seconds each side or until tender. Serve immediately with avocado slices, lime wedges and spring onions.

....
Serves 6

ingredients

> 6 scotch or eye fillet steaks
> 1 avocado, sliced
> lime wedges
> 2 spring onions, sliced

spice mix

> $^1/_2$ onion, very finely chopped
> 3 cloves garlic, crushed
> 1 tablespoon mild chili powder
> 2 teaspoons grated lime rind
> 1 teaspoon ground cumin
> 2 tablespoons olive oil
> 1 tablespoon lime juice

tip from the chef

For a complete meal add warm tortillas, refried beans and a lettuce salad.

a

b

c

16 > ZESTY MEAT

beef
with spinach

a

beef and veal > 17

■ ■ □ | Cooking time: 15 minutes - Preparation time: 25 minutes

method

1. Heat oil in a wok or frying pan, add steak and stir-fry (a) for 3-4 minutes or until browned. Remove meat from pan and drain on absorbent kitchen paper.
2. Add spinach, ginger and garlic to pan (b) and stir-fry for 2-3 minutes or until spinach starts to wilt. Combine cornflour, water, satay sauce, sherry and soy sauce, stir into spinach mixture (c) and cook for 2 minutes or until mixture boils and thickens.
3. Return meat to pan, add cashew nuts (d) and cook for 2-3 minutes or until heated through.

Serves 4

ingredients

- > 2 tablespoons peanut oil
- > 500 g/1 lb lean rump steak, cut into strips
- > 1 bunch/500 g/1 lb spinach, leaves removed and shredded
- > 2 teaspoons grated fresh ginger
- > 2 cloves garlic, crushed
- > 3 teaspoons cornflour
- > 1 cup/250 ml/8 fl oz water
- > 2 tablespoons satay sauce
- > 2 tablespoons dry sherry
- > 1 tablespoon soy sauce
- > 60 g/2 oz roasted cashew nuts

tip from the chef

When buying a wok, choose a large one – with at least a 35 cm/14 in diameter and deep sides. A heavy wok made of carbon steel is better than a light stainless steel or aluminum one. Remember it is easier to cook a small amount of food in a large wok than to cook a large amount of food in a small wok!

b

c

d

18 > ZESTY MEAT

beef
tostada cups

beef and veal > 19

■■□ | Cooking time: 15 minutes - Preparation time: 25 minutes

method

1. Heat oil in a saucepan until a cube of bread dropped in browns in 50 seconds. Deep-fry tortillas, one at a time pressed between two metal ladles, for 1 minute or until crisp and golden. Drain on absorbent kitchen paper.
2. To make filling, place chili powder, cumin and lime juice in a glass or ceramic dish and mix to combine. Add steak, turn to coat and marinate for 5 minutes. Drain steak and cook on a preheated barbecue or under a grill for 2-3 minutes each side or until cooked to your liking. Rest steak for 2 minutes, then cut into strips and place in a bowl. Add onions and coriander leaves and toss to combine.
3. To serve, divide filling between tostada cups and serve immediately.

ingredients

> **vegetable oil for deep-frying**
> **8 corn tortillas**

beef filling

> **2 teaspoons mild chili powder**
> **1 teaspoon ground cumin**
> **1/4 cup/60 ml/2 fl oz lime juice**
> **500 g/1 lb rump steak, trimmed of visible fat**
> **2 red onions, sliced**
> **1/2 bunch coriander**

Makes 8

tip from the chef

Serve these tasty snacks with salsas of your choice and lime wedges.

> ZESTY MEAT

cocktail meatballs

■ ☐ ☐ | Cooking time: 5 minutes - Preparation time: 25 minutes

ingredients

meatballs
> 250 g/8 oz minced beef
> 1 onion, grated
> 2 tablespoons dried breadcrumbs
> 1/2 teaspoon salt
> 1 egg
> 1 tablespoon chopped parsley
> 1/4 teaspoon pepper
> 1/4 teaspoon oregano
> 1 teaspoon Tabasco sauce

filling
> 8 prunes, pitted and chopped
> 1 tablespoon pine nuts, coarsely chopped

for glazing
> Worcestershire sauce

method

1. Mix mince and all ingredients for meatballs together (a), knead well with hands until mince becomes fine in grain. Allow to stand for 15 minutes before rolling.
2. Combine prunes and pine nuts. Wet palms of hands to prevent mince sticking, take about a tablespoon of mince, roll into a ball then flatten in palm of hand.
3. Place 1/2 teaspoon of filling in center and remould into a smooth ball (b). Space around edge of large dinner plate, glaze meatballs with Worcestershire sauce.
4. Cook in microwave on High for 5 minutes (c). Cover with foil and stand 1 1/2 minutes.
5. Serve with a spicy plum dipping sauce.

Makes 16 small meatballs

tip from the chef

Dried apricots or raisins may be used instead of prunes and walnuts, and almonds in place of pine nuts. You can also make the meatballs without the stuffing, but cook 4 minutes only. Serve with tomato sauce.

a

beef and veal > 21

b

c

super steak sandwiches

beef and veal > 23

■□□ | Cooking time: 10 minutes - Preparation time: 20 minutes

method
1. Heat oil in a frying pan over a high heat, add onions and cook, stirring, for 2-3 minutes or until onions are soft. Push onions to side of pan, add steaks and pineapple rings and cook for 2 minutes each side or until steak is cooked to your liking.
2. Top 4 slices of toast each with a slice of cheese, 2 slices tomato, a lettuce leaf, a steak, some onions, a pineapple ring, a spoonful of tomato or barbecue sauce and remaining toast slices. Serve immediately.

Serves 4

ingredients
> 2 teaspoons vegetable oil
> 2 onions, chopped
> 4 small lean rump steaks
> 4 canned pineapple rings, drained
> 8 thick slices wholemeal bread, toasted
> 4 slices tasty cheese (mature Cheddar)
> 8 slices tomato
> 4 lettuce leaves
> tomato or barbecue sauce

tip from the chef
Steak sandwiches can also be cooked on the barbecue; rather than cooking in a frying pan cook on a lightly oiled preheated medium barbecue plate. Serve with oven fries or potatoes and coleslaw.

> ZESTY MEAT

rack of veal on mashed potatoes

■ □ □ | Cooking time: 45 minutes - Preparation time: 25 minutes

ingredients
- 750 g/1½ lb potatoes, peeled and chopped
- 120 ml/4 fl oz olive oil
- 1 tablespoon capers, chopped
- 2 tablespoons roasted garlic purée
- salt
- freshly ground black pepper
- 2 tablespoons olive oil
- 1 kg/2 lb rack of veal (8 points)
- 2 tablespoons thyme leaves
- 300 ml/10 fl oz white wine
- 300 ml/10 fl oz veal or chicken stock

method
1. Preheat oven at 180°C/350°F/Gas 4. Boil the potatoes until soft. Drain, then mash (or purée), and add the olive oil, chopped capers and half the roasted garlic. Mix well, season with salt and pepper to taste and set aside until ready to serve.
2. Heat olive oil in a pan, and brown the veal on both sides until well sealed. This will take approximately 5 minutes. Remove the veal from the pan, and place on a rack in a baking dish. Rub the veal with remaining roasted garlic and 1 tablespoon of thyme leaves. Season with salt and pepper, add half the wine and stock to the baking dish.
3. Roast in the oven for 20 minutes or until veal is cooked to your liking. Wrap in foil and let rest for 10 minutes.
4. Add remaining stock, wine and thyme to the pan-juices and cook over a medium heat for 5 minutes or until the liquid has reduced by a third.
5. Serve the veal on a bed of mashed potatoes with pan-juices.

Serves 4

tip from the chef
A rack of veal may be replaced by a rack of lamb.

beef and veal > 25

> ZESTY MEAT

carpetburgers
with caper

beef and veal

mayonnaise

■ ■ □ | Cooking time: 15 minutes - Preparation time: 25 minutes

method

1. Place beef, sausage meat, spring onions, garlic, lemon rind and dill in a bowl and mix to combine. Shape mixture into twelve patties.
2. Top half the patties with 3 oysters each (a), then, with the remaining patties, pinch edges together to join and completely seal the filling. Wrap a piece of bacon around each pattie and secure with wooden toothpicks or cocktail sticks (b).
3. Place wine and oil in a large shallow glass or ceramic dish and mix to combine. Add patties and marinate for 10 minutes.
4. Drain patties and cook on a preheated medium barbecue for 5-7 minutes each side or until cooked.
5. To make mayonnaise, place mayonnaise, cream, capers, lemon rind and gherkin in a bowl and mix to combine. Serve with patties.

Serves 6

ingredients

> 500 g/1 lb lean ground beef
> 250 g/8 oz sausage meat
> 4 spring onions, finely chopped
> 2 cloves garlic, crushed
> 2 teaspoons finely grated lemon rind
> 1 teaspoon finely chopped fresh dill
> 18 bottled oysters
> 3 rashers bacon, cut in half lengthwise and rind removed
> 2 tablespoons red wine
> 2 tablespoons olive oil

caper mayonnaise
> 2 tablespoons mayonnaise
> 1/2 cup/125 ml/4 fl oz cream (double)
> 2 teaspoons chopped capers
> 1 teaspoon finely grated lemon rind
> 1 small gherkin, finely chopped

tip from the chef

A more economical, but just as tasty variation on that old favorite carpetbag steak. Prunes, dried apricots or sliced cheese can be used in place of the oysters.

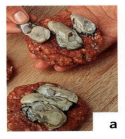
a

b

veal chops with sun-dried tomatoes

beef and veal > 29

■■☐ | Cooking time: 45 minutes - Preparation time: 30 minutes

method
1. Coat chops with flour. Melt butter in a frying pan and cook garlic, prosciutto and rosemary over a high heat for 2 minutes. Add chops and brown on both sides.
2. Stir in wine. Bring to the boil, reduce heat and simmer for 30 minutes or until veal is cooked.
3. Remove chops and prosciutto from pan and set aside to keep warm. Increase heat, stir in tomatoes and cook until sauce is reduced by half. Stir in basil and spoon sauce over chops and top with prosciutto.

ingredients
> 8 veal chops, trimmed of all visible fat
> seasoned flour
> 60 g/2 oz butter
> 1 clove garlic, crushed
> 6 slices prosciutto, chopped
> 2 tablespoons chopped fresh rosemary
> 250 ml/8 fl oz dry white wine
> 16 sun-dried tomatoes, chopped
> 4 tablespoons chopped fresh basil

Serves 4

tip from the chef
Sun-dried tomatoes are becoming increasingly popular and are available from most delicatessens.

four serving plates. Sprinkle with Parmesan cheese.
2. To make mayonnaise, place egg, lemon juice, garlic and mustard in a food processor or blender and process to combine. With machine running, slowly add oil and continue processing until mayonnaise thickens. Season to taste with black pepper. Spoon a little mayonnaise over salad and serve immediately.

separated and washed
> 1 bunch/250 g/8 oz watercress
> 90 g/3 oz Parmesan cheese, grated

mustard mayonnaise
> 1 egg
> 1 tablespoon lemon juice
> 2 cloves garlic, crushed
> 2 teaspoons Dijon mustard
> 1/2 cup/125 ml/4 fl oz olive oil
> freshly ground black pepper

Serves 4

tip from the chef
To achieve very thin slices of beef, wrap the fillet in plastic food wrap and place in the freezer for 15 minutes or until firm, then slice using a very sharp knife.

carpaccio with mustard mayonnaise

beef fillet wrapped in pastry

Cooking time: 60 minutes - Preparation time: 70 minutes

method

1. Melt half the butter in a large frying pan. When sizzling, add fillet and cook over a medium heat (a) for 10 minutes, turning to brown and seal all sides. Remove meat from pan and set aside to cool completely.
2. Melt remaining butter in frying pan and cook onion for 5 minutes or until soft. Add mushrooms (b) and cook, stirring, for 15 minutes or until mushrooms give up all their juices and these have evaporated. Season to taste with black pepper and nutmeg, stir in parsley and set aside to cool completely.
3. Roll out pastry to a length 10 cm/4 in longer than meat and wide enough to wrap around fillet. Spread half the mushroom mixture down center of pastry and place fillet on top. Spread remaining mushroom mixture on top of fillet. Cut out corners of pastry. Brush pastry edges with egg. Wrap pastry around fillet (c) like a parcel, tucking in ends (d). Place pastry-wrapped fillet seam side down on a lightly greased baking sheet and freeze for 10 minutes.

ingredients

- 60 g/2 oz butter
- 1 kg/2 lb fillet steak, in one piece, trimmed of all visible fat
- 1 onion, chopped
- 375 g/12 oz button mushrooms, finely chopped
- freshly ground black pepper
- pinch ground nutmeg
- 1 tablespoon chopped fresh parsley
- 500 g/1 lb prepared puff pastry
- 1 egg, lightly beaten

red wine sauce

- 1 cup/250 ml/8 fl oz red wine
- 1 teaspoon finely chopped fresh thyme or $1/4$ teaspoon dried thyme
- 1 teaspoon finely chopped fresh parsley
- 100 g/$3^{1}/_{2}$ oz butter, cut into small pieces
- 2 teaspoons cornflour blended with 1 tablespoon water

a

b

beef fillet wrapped in pastry

4. Roll out remaining pastry to 10 x 30 cm/ 4 x 12 in length and cut into strips 1 cm/^{1}/$_2$ in wide. Remove fillet from freezer and brush pastry all over with egg. Arrange 5 pastry strips diagonally over pastry parcel, then arrange remaining strips diagonally in opposite direction. Brush only top of strips with egg and bake at 220°C/425°F/Gas 7 for 30 minutes for medium-rare beef. Place on a warmed serving platter and set aside to rest in a warm place for 10 minutes.

5. To make sauce, place wine in a small saucepan and cook over a medium heat until reduced by half. Add thyme, parsley and black pepper to taste. Remove pan from heat and quickly whisk in one piece of butter at a time, ensuring that each piece is completely whisked in and melted before adding the next. Whisk in cornflour mixture and cook over a medium heat, stirring until sauce thickens. Serve with sliced beef.

....
Serves 6

tip from the chef
To wrap the meat, make a pastry shell with 150 g/5oz butter, 1 egg, 300 g/10 oz flour, 2 tablespoons cold water and salt.

c

d

beef and veal > 35

wellington bread loaf

ZESTY MEAT

wellington bread loaf

■■□ | Cooking time: 90 minutes - Preparation time: 35 minutes

ingredients
- 1 Vienna loaf
- 30 g/1 oz butter, melted
- 250 g/8 oz liver pâté
- 125 g/4 oz button mushrooms, sliced
- 750 g/1 1/2 lb lean beef mince
- 2 tablespoons snipped fresh chives
- 2 teaspoons crushed black peppercorns
- 2 eggs, lightly beaten
- 1/2 beef stock cube
- 1 tablespoon tomato paste (purée)

red wine and thyme sauce
- 30 g/1 oz butter
- 2 tablespoons flour
- 1/2 cup/125 ml/4 fl oz beef stock
- 1/2 cup/125 ml/4 fl oz dry red wine
- freshly ground black pepper

method
1. Cut base from bread loaf and reserve. Scoop bread from center of loaf leaving a 1 cm/1/2 in shell. Make bread from center into crumbs and set aside (a), brush inside of bread shell with butter, spread with pâté, then press mushroom slices into pâté.
2. Place 1/4 cup/60 g/2 oz reserved breadcrumbs (keep remaining breadcrumbs for another use), beef, chives, black peppercorns, eggs, stock cube and tomato paste (purée) in a bowl and mix to combine.
3. Spoon beef mixture into bread shell (b), packing down well. Reposition base and wrap loaf in aluminum foil. Place loaf on a baking tray and bake at 180°C/350°F/Gas4 for 1 1/2 hours or until meat mixture is cooked.

a

b

beef and veal

4. To make sauce, melt butter in a saucepan over a medium heat. Stir in flour and cook, stirring, for 1 minute. Remove pan from heat and gradually whisk in stock and wine (c). Return pan to heat and cook, stirring constantly, for 4-5 minutes or until sauce boils and thickens. Season with black pepper to taste. Serve sauce with meatloaf.

....
Serves 8

tip from the chef

Breadcrumbs are easy to make, simply put the bread in a food processor and process to make crumbs; if you do not have a food processor rub the bread through a sieve. It is preferable for the breadcrumbs to be made with stale bread; for this recipe either use a loaf of bread that is a day or two old or scoop out the center of the loaf as described in the recipe, then spread the bread out on a tray and leave for 2-3 hours to become stale, before making into crumbs.

c

pork with mango couscous

■ ■ □ | Cooking time: 2 hours - Preparation time: 40 minutes

ingredients

> 1 1/2 kg/3 lb boneless pork loin, rind removed and trimmed of all visible fat

mango couscous stuffing
> 1/2 cup/90 g/3 oz couscous
> 1/2 cup/125 ml/4 fl oz boiling water
> 1/2 mango, chopped
> 2 spring onions, chopped
> 3 tablespoons chopped fresh coriander
> 2 teaspoons finely grated lime rind
> 1/2 teaspoon garam masala
> 1 egg white, lightly beaten
> 1 tablespoon lime juice

creamy wine sauce
> 1/2 cup/125 ml/4 fl oz chicken stock
> 1/2 cup/125 ml/4 fl oz white wine
> 2 tablespoons natural yogurt

method

1. To make stuffing, place couscous in a bowl, pour over boiling water and toss with a fork until couscous absorbs all the liquid. Add mango, spring onions, coriander, lime rind, garam masala (a), egg white and lime juice and mix to combine.
2. Lay pork out flat and spread stuffing evenly over surface (b). Roll up firmly and secure with string (c). Place pork on a wire rack set in a roasting tin, pour in 2 1/2 cm/1 in water and bake at 190°C/375°F/Gas 5 for 1 1/2 hours or until pork is cooked to your liking. Place pork on a serving platter, set aside and keep warm.
3. To make sauce, skim excess fat from pan juices, stir in stock and wine and bring to the boil over a medium heat. Reduce heat and simmer for 10 minutes or until sauce reduces by half. Remove tin from heat and whisk in yogurt. Slice pork and serve with sauce.

Serves 8

tip from the chef

On completion of cooking, remove meat from oven, cover and stand in a warm place for 10-15 minutes before carving. Standing allows the juices to settle and makes carving easier.

a

pork > 39

b

c

roast pork
with apple stuffing

pork > 41

■■■ | Cooking time: 90 minutes - Preparation time: 40 minutes

method
1. Using a sharp knife, make a pocket in the pork by separating bones from meat, leaving both ends intact.
2. To make stuffing, melt butter in a frying pan and cook apple for 2-3 minutes or until soft. Remove pan from heat and stir in breadcrumbs, lemon rind, allspice, apple jelly and sultanas.
3. Pack mixture into pocket in pork and place on a roasting rack in a baking dish. Rub rind of pork with salt and bake at 250°C/500°F/Gas 9 for 20 minutes. Reduce heat to 190°C/375°F/Gas 5 and bake for 1 hour longer or until meat is cooked through. Stand for 10 minutes before carving.

ingredients
- 1.5 kg/3 lb loin of pork, with bone in and rind scored
- 1 tablespoon salt

apple stuffing
- 30 g/1 oz butter
- 1 green apple, cored, peeled and finely chopped
- 60 g/2 oz breadcrumbs, made from stale bread
- 1 teaspoon finely grated lemon rind
- 1 teaspoon ground allspice
- 1 tablespoon apple jelly
- 3 tablespoons sultanas

....
Serves 6

tip from the chef
So that pork will not result hard to digest, make sure the meat is well done and all the fat has been removed. Sage is an herb that combines with this type of meat, making the roast more easily digestible.

spiced pork fillet

■□□ | Cooking time: 40 minutes - Preparation time: 5 minutes

ingredients
- 500 g/1 lb pork fillets
- 1/2 cup/125 ml/4 fl oz chicken stock
- 2 teaspoons cornflour

ginger marinade
- 2 tablespoons hoisin sauce
- 1 tablespoon soy sauce
- 2 teaspoons vinegar
- 2 tablespoons dry sherry
- 1 teaspoon grated fresh ginger
- 2 tablespoons honey

method
1. Place pork fillets in a shallow glass or ceramic dish. To make marinade, place hoisin sauce, soy sauce, vinegar, sherry, ginger and honey in a small bowl, mix to combine. Pour marinade over pork, cover and set aside to marinate for 1 hour.
2. Drain pork and reserve marinade. Place pork in a baking dish and bake at 180°C/350°F/Gas 4 for 30 minutes, turning several times.
3. Place reserved marinade, stock and cornflour in a saucepan and cook, stirring, until sauce boils and thickens. To serve, slice pork and spoon sauce over slices.

Serves 4

tip from the chef
Hoisin sauce, sometimes called Chinese barbecue sauce, is a thick, brownish red sauce made from soy beans, vinegar, sugar, spices and other flavorings. It is used both in cooking and as a condiment.

pork > 43

chinese spareribs

■ ☐ ☐ | Cooking time: 60 minutes - Preparation time: 5 minutes

method
1. Cut each sparerib into 3 pieces and place in a bowl. Combine sherry, honey, plum sauce, tomato sauce, chilies, garlic, ginger and five spice powder and pour over ribs. Mix well to coat ribs.
2. Place ribs and sauce mixture in a large frying pan, cover and cook over a low heat, stirring occasionally, for 1 hour or until pork is tender and glazed.

Serves 4

ingredients
- 8 pork spareribs, trimmed of rind and excess fat
- 1/4 cup/60 ml/2 fl oz dry sherry
- 2 tablespoons honey
- 2 tablespoons plum sauce
- 1/4 cup/60 ml/2 fl oz tomato sauce
- 2 fresh red chilies, seeded and chopped
- 2 cloves garlic, crushed
- 1 tablespoon grated fresh ginger
- 1/2 teaspoon five spice powder

tip from the chef
Plum sauce is available from Asian food shops and most supermarkets. Made from dried plums, apricots, vinegar, sugar and spices, it is a thick, sweet chutney-like sauce that is used as a condiment.

46 > ZESTY MEAT

pork with
mole and dumplings

■■■ | Cooking time: 90 minutes - Preparation time: 70 minutes

ingredients

> 1 kg/2 lb pork cutlets, trimmed of visible fat
> 1/2 onion
> 2 cloves garlic
> 315 g/10 oz green beans
> 315 g/10 oz zucchini, chopped

mole amarillo

> 2 ancho chilies
> 4 guajillo chilies
> 250 g/8 oz canned tomatillos, drained and peeled
> 1 tomato
> 6 garlic cloves
> 2 tablespoons ground coriander
> 2 black peppercorns
> 1 clove
> 1/2 teaspoon ground cumin
> 1 tablespoon vegetable oil

masa dumplings

> 500 g/1 lb fresh masa
> 60 g/2 oz butter or lard

tip from the chef

Mole means sauce and as such you will find hundreds in Mexican cooking. Believed to have originated from the states of Oaxaca and Puebla, one of the most famous moles is mole poblano.

method

1. Place pork, onion and garlic in a saucepan and pour over enough cold water to cover. Bring to simmering over a medium heat and simmer, skimming the surface occasionally, for 50 minutes or until pork is tender.
2. Add beans and zucchini and simmer for 5 minutes, then remove pork and vegetables. Strain cooking liquid and reserve.
3. To make mole, place chilies in a bowl, cover with hot water and soak for 20 minutes or until soft. Drain chilies and place them in a hot frying pan or comal and cook until skins are blistered and charred. Set aside until cool then remove seeds.
4. Process chilies, tomatillos, tomato, garlic, coriander, peppercorns, clove and cumin to make a purée. Push purée through a sieve.
5. Heat oil in a frying pan over a medium heat, add purée and cook, stirring, for 8 minutes. Stir in 6 cups/1.5 litres/2¹/2 pt of the reserved cooking liquid, bring to simmering and simmer for 10 minutes.
6. To make dumplings, place masa and butter or lard in a bowl and knead to combine (a). Divide dough into 24 pieces and roll into small flat balls. Make a thumb print in each dumpling (b) to about halfway through. Add dumplings to mole and cook, stirring gently, for 8-10 minutes or until dumplings are tender. Add pork and vegetables and simmer for 4 minutes or until heated through.

Serves 6

pork > 47

balsamic
pork stir-fry

pork > 49

■□□ | Cooking time: 7 minutes - Preparation time: 35 minutes

method

1. Heat oil in a wok over a high heat, add garlic and stir-fry for 1 minute or until golden. Add pork and stir-fry for 3 minutes or until brown. Add red pepper, green pepper, orange juice and vinegar and stir-fry for 3 minutes or until pork is cooked. Season to taste with black pepper.
2. Divide rocket or watercress between serving plates, then top with pork mixture. Serve immediately.

Serves 4

ingredients

> 2 teaspoons olive oil
> 2 cloves garlic, crushed
> 500 g/1 lb pork fillet, trimmed of all visible fat, cut into 1 cm/^{1}/$_2$ in thick slices
> 1 red pepper, chopped
> 1 green pepper, chopped
> ^{1}/$_2$ cup/125 ml/4 fl oz orange juice
> ^{1}/$_4$ cup/60 ml/2 fl oz balsamic vinegar
> freshly ground black pepper
> 1 bunch/125 g/4 oz rocket or watercress leaves

tip from the chef

Balsamic vinegar is a dark red wine vinegar. Once a delicatessen item, in recent years it has become increasingly popular and can now be purchased from many supermarkets.

honey-glazed spareribs

■■□ | Cooking time: 30 minutes - Preparation time: 40 minutes

ingredients

- 2 kg/4 lb pork spareribs, trimmed of excess fat
- 2 onions, chopped
- 2 tablespoons fresh parsley, chopped
- 1 cup/250 ml/8 fl oz chicken stock
- 2 tablespoons lemon juice
- 125 g/4 oz butter, melted

honey-soy marinade

- 4 small fresh red chilies, chopped
- 4 cloves garlic, chopped
- 2 spring onions, chopped
- 1 tablespoon fresh ginger, finely grated
- 1 1/2 cups/375 ml/12 fl oz rice-wine vinegar
- 1/2 cup/125 ml/4 fl oz reduced-salt soy sauce
- 1/2 cup/170 g/5 1/2 oz honey

method

1. To make marinade, combine chilies, garlic, spring onions, ginger, vinegar, soy sauce and honey in a non-reactive dish. Add ribs, toss to coat, cover and marinate in the refrigerator for at least 4 hours.
2. Drain ribs and reserve marinade. Cook ribs, basting occasionally with reserved marinade, on a preheated hot barbecue grill for 8-10 minutes or until ribs are tender and golden. Place on a serving platter, cover and keep warm.
3. Place remaining marinade in a saucepan, add onions, parsley, stock and lemon juice and bring to the boil. Reduce heat and simmer for 15 minutes or until sauce reduces by half. Pour mixture into a food processor or blender and process to make a purée. With motor running, pour in hot melted butter and process to combine. Serve sauce with spareribs.

Serves 8

tip from the chef

Pork chops in their marinade should be served steaming hot.

pork > 51

52 > ZESTY MEAT

pork > 53

chili meat pattie casserole

■■■ | Cooking time: 45 minutes - Preparation time: 50 minutes

method

1. Place pork, taco seasoning mix, egg, breadcrumbs and half the cheese in a bowl and mix to combine. Shape meat and mixture into patties.

2. Heat 2 tablespoons oil in a nonstick frying pan over a medium heat, add patties and cook for 3-4 minutes each side or until brown. Place patties in a shallow ovenproof dish and set aside.

3. Heat 1 tablespoon oil in pan over a medium heat, add onion, chili and garlic and cook, stirring, for 3-4 minutes or until onion is soft. Stir in tomatoes, salsa and tomato paste (purée) and bring to the boil. Reduce heat and simmer for 5 minutes. Pour sauce over meat patties.

4. To make topping, boil, steam or microwave potatoes until just tender. Drain and refresh under cold running water. Peel potatoes and grate coarsely. Place potatoes, eggs and corn chips in a bowl and mix to combine.

5. Heat 2 tablespoons oil in a large frying pan over a medium heat and cook spoonfuls of potato mixture for 3-4 minutes each side or until golden. Remove from pan, drain on absorbent kitchen paper and place slightly overlapping on top of patties, sprinkle with remaining cheese and bake at 180°C/350°F/Gas 4 for 15 minutes.

Serves 4

ingredients

> 500 g/1 lb lean ground pork
> 2 tablespoons taco seasoning mix
> 1 egg
> 3/4 cup/45 g/1 1/2 oz breadcrumbs, made from stale bread
> 250 g/8 oz tasty cheese (mature Cheddar), grated
> vegetable oil
> 1 onion, finely chopped
> 1 small fresh red chili, finely chopped
> 2 cloves garlic, crushed
> 440 g/14 oz canned tomatoes, undrained and mashed
> 1/2 cup/125 ml/4 fl oz bottled tomato salsa
> 1 1/2 tablespoons tomato paste (purée)

hash brown topping
> 2 large potatoes, scrubbed
> 2 eggs, lightly beaten
> 155 g/5 oz packet corn chips, crushed

tip from the chef

Topping may be replaced with a rösti potato crunch (grated potatoes pan-fried Swiss style).

54 > ZESTY MEAT

chargrilled lamb
with mint pesto

■■□ | Cooking time: 60 minutes - Preparation time: 25 minutes

ingredients

> **4 lamb backstraps (450 g/1 lb in total)**
> **salt and freshly ground black pepper**

creamy potatoes

> **500 g/1 lb potatoes, thinly sliced**
> **salt and freshly ground black pepper**
> **1 garlic clove, crushed**
> **1 teaspoon nutmeg**
> **1 tablespoon plain flour**
> **1/3 cup/40 g/1 1/3 oz Parmesan cheese, grated**
> **1 cup/250 ml/8 fl oz cream**
> **2 tablespoons Parmesan cheese, grated (extra)**

mint pesto

> **1 cup/60 g/2 oz mint leaves**
> **1/2 cup/30 g/1 oz parsley leaves**
> **2 cloves garlic**
> **1/2 cup/90 g/3 oz pine nuts, toasted**
> **3 tablespoons Parmesan cheese, grated**
> **3 tablespoons pecorino cheese, grated**
> **1/3 cup/85 ml/2 1/2 fl oz olive oil**

method

1. Preheat oven at 180°C/350°F/Gas 4. Season lamb with salt and freshly ground pepper to taste and set aside.
2. Lightly grease an ovenproof dish with butter and arrange the potato slices in overlapping rows in the dish, seasoning between each layer with salt and pepper, garlic and nutmeg.
3. Mix the flour and Parmesan cheese into the cream and pour over the potatoes. Sprinkle with extra Parmesan cheese, then bake for 40-45 minutes or until potatoes are cooked.
4. To make the pesto: place the mint, parsley, garlic, pine nuts and cheeses in the bowl of a food processor, and process until finely chopped. Add the olive oil in a steady stream with the processor still running. Season with salt and pepper then set aside.
5. Preheat the chargrill plate (or pan), and grease lightly with a little oil. Chargrill the lamb on both sides for approximately 5-10 minutes or until done to your liking.
6. Serve the lamb sliced diagonally, on a bed of creamy potatoes with the mint pesto.

Serves 4-6

tip from the chef

Mint goes perfect with lamb. And green mint is the most suitable for this recipe.

lamb > 55

56 > ZESTY MEAT

thai lamb and noodle salad

lamb > 57

■ ■ ■ | Cooking time: 25 minutes - Preparation time: 45 minutes

method

1. Combine lemon grass, garlic, lime juice, oil, chili sauce and fish sauce in a glass or ceramic dish and mix to combine. Add lamb, turn to coat, cover and marinate in the refrigerator for 3 hours.

2. Preheat barbecue to a medium heat. To make salad, prepare noodles according to packet directions. Drain and place in a bowl. Add spring onions, red pepper, bean sprouts and coriander and toss to combine. Set aside.

3. To make dressing, place lime juice, fish sauce, honey and chili powder in a screwtop jar and shake well to combine. Set aside.

4. Drain lamb and cook on lightly oiled barbecue, turning several times, for 5-10 minutes or until cooked to your liking. Slice lamb diagonally into 2 cm/3/4 in thick slices.

5. To serve, place salad on a large serving platter, arrange lamb attractively on top and drizzle with dressing. Serve immediately.

....
Serves 6

ingredients

> **1 stalk fresh lemon grass, chopped or 1/2 teaspoon dried lemon grass, soaked in hot water until soft**
> **2 cloves garlic, crushed**
> **1/4 cup/60 ml/2 fl oz lime juice**
> **2 tablespoons vegetable oil**
> **2 tablespoons sweet chili sauce**
> **1 tablespoon fish sauce**
> **750 g/1 1/2 lb lamb fillets, trimmed of excess fat and sinew**

rice noodle salad

> **155 g/5 oz rice noodles**
> **6 spring onions, chopped**
> **1 red pepper, chopped**
> **60 g/2 oz bean sprouts**
> **3 tablespoons fresh coriander leaves**

lime and chili dressing

> **1/4 cup/60 ml/2 fl oz lime juice**
> **1 tablespoon fish sauce**
> **1 tablespoon honey**
> **pinch chili powder or according to taste**

tip from the chef

Rice noodles vary in size from a narrow vermicelli style to a ribbon noodle about 5 mm/1/4 in wide. They should be soaked before using: the narrow noodles require about 10 minutes soaking, while the wider ones will need about 30 minutes.

> ZESTY MEAT

crispy lamb tortilla pizza

Cooking time: 3 hours - Preparation time: 50 minutes

ingredients
> 500 g/1 lb fresh masa
> 315 g/10 oz beans, cooked and mashed
> 315 g/10 oz feta cheese, crumbled
> 1 cup/250 ml/8 fl oz enchilada sauce
> lime wedges
> chopped fresh chilies

twice cooked lamb
> 1.5 kg/3 lb leg lamb
> 1 onion, halved
> 2 cloves garlic
> 3 sprigs fresh oregano
> 1/2 teaspoon cumin seeds
> chili powder

method
1. To cook lamb, place lamb, onion, garlic, oregano and cumin seeds in a saucepan and pour over enough water to cover. Bring to the boil, cover, reduce heat and simmer for 1 1/2 hours or until very tender. Drain lamb and place in a baking dish. Sprinkle with chili powder and bake at 180°C/350°F/Gas 4 for 30 minutes. Shred lamb and set aside.
2. Take 4 tablespoons masa, place between sheets of nonstick baking paper and roll out to form a large, very thin round. Place tortilla in a hot dry frying pan or comal and cook for 3 minutes each side or until crisp. Keep warm while cooking remaining tortillas.
3. Spread tortillas with beans, then top with shredded lamb, feta cheese and enchilada sauce and bake for 10 minutes or until topping is heated through. Serve with lime wedges and chopped chilies.

Serves 4

tip from the chef
Fresh masa and enchilada sauce can be purchased from Mexican specialty food stores or wholesalers.

lamb > 59

barbecued
lamb pitta breads

lamb > 61

■ □ □ | Cooking time: 12 minutes - Preparation time: 25 minutes

method
1. Combine lemon rind, cumin and oil. Rub surface of lamb with oil mixture. Place in a shallow glass or ceramic dish and marinate at room temperature for 30 minutes.
2. Preheat barbecue to a medium heat. Place lamb on lightly oiled barbecue grill and cook for 3-5 minutes each side or until lamb is tender and cooked to your liking.
3. Warm pitta breads on barbecue for 1-2 minutes each side. Split each pitta bread to make a pocket, then spread with hummus and fill with endive, tabbouleh and sliced lamb.

ingredients
- 1 tablespoon finely grated lemon rind
- 1 teaspoon ground cumin
- 1 tablespoon olive oil
- 750 g/1 １/2 lb lamb fillets
- 6 pitta bread rounds
- 6 tablespoons ready-made hummus
- 1 bunch curly endive
- 250 g/8 oz ready-made tabbouleh

Serves 6

tip from the chef
For extra flavor serve with a spoonful of your favorite chutney.

slow-baked chili lamb

■□□ | Cooking time: 1-2 hours - Preparation time: 1 hour

ingredients

> 1.5 kg/3 lb leg lamb, trimmed of visible fat

chili herb paste

> 4 ancho chilies
> 3 cloves garlic, unpeeled
> 1 ripe tomato, peeled and chopped
> 1 tablespoon chopped fresh oregano
> 1/2 teaspoon ground cumin
> 1/2 teaspoon crushed black peppercorns
> 2 tablespoons apple cider vinegar

method

1. To make chili paste, place chilies and garlic in a hot dry frying pan or comal over a high heat and cook until skins are blistered and charred. Place chilies in a bowl, pour over hot water to cover and soak for 30 minutes. Drain chilies and discard water.
2. Squeeze garlic from skins. Place chilies, garlic, tomato, oregano, cumin, peppercorns and vinegar in a food processor or blender and process to make a purée.
3. Place lamb in a glass or ceramic dish, spread with chili paste, cover and marinate in the refrigerator for at least 3 hours or overnight.
4. Transfer lamb to a baking dish and roast in oven at 150°C/300°F/Gas 2 for 1-2 hours or until tender.

Serves 6

tip from the chef

Slice lamb and serve with warm tortillas, vegetables and a selection of salsas.

lamb > 63

World Wide Publication & Distribution:

STANDARD INTERNATIONAL MEDIA HOLDINGS

www.standardinternationalmedia.com

Chef Express Ultimate Collection Family Meals

Chef Express™ Creative Chicken, Family Meals, My First Cookbook, Pasta Supreme, Take 20 Minutes!, Zesty Meat

© STANDARD INTERNATIONAL COPYRIGHT LEASING

Publisher
Simon St. John Bailey

Editor-in-chief
Susan Knightley

Prepress
Precision Prep & Press

Printing
Tara TPS Korea

All rights reserved. No part of this book may be stored, reproduced or transmitted in any form and by any means without written permission of the Publisher, except in the case of brief quotations embodied in critical articles and reviews.

ISBN 9781600819759

2014